Resin Jewellery

Techniques & projects
inspired by the history of
art, craft and jewellery

THREE GABLES
Publishing

Resin
Jewellery

Clare John

To my grandmother Marianne Hellwig-Blaauw
artist, sculptor, ceramicist, jeweller
1905-1946

First published
in Great Britain in 2014
Three Gables Publishing
Gloucestershire

ISBN: 978-0-9926473-0-8

Copyright © 2014 Clare John

All images: Copyright © 2014
Clare John and individual artists

A CIP catalogue record for
this book is available from the
British Library.

. . . .

Disclaimer
The projects in this book are intended for the personal use
of the reader and may be reproduced for that purpose only.
Any other use, especially commercial use, is forbidden under
law without written permission of the author.

We have made every effort to ensure that all technical
information is correct at the time of going to press. But we
cannot be held responsible for any injury, loss or damage
to either persons or property. Read through all health and
safety information and check the information specific to the
materials you use. Health and safety information is usually
available from the suppliers and their websites.

We recommend that children do not use resin and advise you
to keep all materials out of reach of children and animals.

. . . .

Previous page:
Clare John Plique a jour Bracelet 2010
Silver and resin

Opposite:
Clare John Resin Mosaic Bracelet 2014
Silver-plated metal and resin

Page 137:
Clare John Square Bracelet 2014
Silver-plated metal, sequins, beads, Angelina fibre and resin

Photograph credits
Step-by-step photos by Clare John.
Finished jewellery photos by Paul Mounsey.

Artwork and design by Sarah John.
Photo editing by Charlotte Stevens.

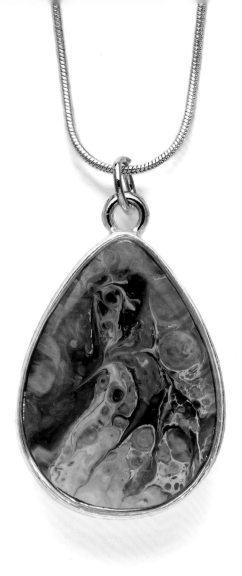

Green Teardrop Pendant 2014 *Silver plated pendant and resin*

Contents

projects

Acknowledgements and thanks

To my husband, Rob Small; my parents, David John and Marianne Hellwig John; my sisters, Helen John Prior, Rachel John and Sarah John Wilson; my brother, Simon John; my sister-in-law, Noleen John; my son, James Small and my daughter, Ellen Small and my nephew, Joshua John. Thank you for all the help and inspiration.

To my models Rob Small, Helen John Prior, Ellen Small, Ann May Jenkins and Juliana Jenkins.

To Marianne Hellwig John, MaggieJo St John, Kate Battes and Julia West for your editorial help.

To the British Museum and the Victoria and Albert Museum, London for inspiration and permission to use images from your collections.

To Joan Gordon and Sian Hamilton – great editors at *My Creative-Diva* and *Making Jewellery* magazine.

To Lisa Cain and Tim McCreight for being such inspiring teachers.

To Erv Johnson for advice on writing books.

To Kate Battes for your help in running the business while I was writing this book.

And to Ron Bright, Mandy Bryon and Jenny Deacon at RF Bright Enterprises Ltd for your great products, endless support and technical help.

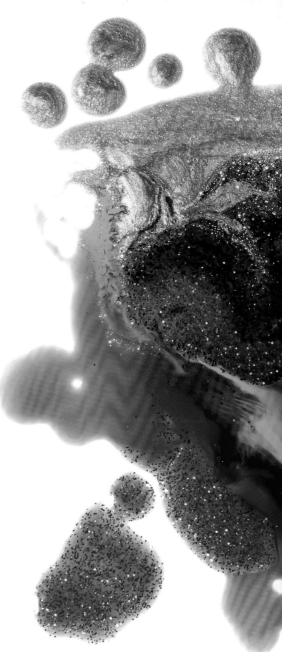

Introduction

Colour, texture, sparkle, metallic effects, precious mementoes embedded in clear resin, chunky castings that are not heavy; **welcome to the world of resin.**

Beginners as well as more advanced makers can use this book. The resin part of the majority of the projects can be used in ready-made jewellery mounts. You will find that the jewellery making section will require different skill levels. Each project has skill level and estimated making time indicated.

I started using resin in jewellery in the 1970s, when I was studying for my B.A. in Silversmithing. I wanted to add colour to silver pieces and I fell in love with the vivid colours I could get with resin, a material that did not need a kiln or expensive equipment. Resin is amazing and has developed in leaps and bounds since the 1970s. There are no longer highly dangerous, strong smelling materials and the hit or miss has gone from the process. Modern resins also set with a hard, shiny surface so there is no more rubbing down and polishing.

Landscape Rings 1976 Silver and resin

Resin Pendant 2014 *Resin and elastic bands*

I have been teaching resin workshops since 2004 and I am always delighted by the excitement and pleasure students get from the colour, texture and high quality finishes they learn to achieve with resin, in a very short time. It is this excitement that I want to share with you.

Inspiration for creative work can come from many sources: nature, architecture, art, photography and the work of other artists. In this book I have drawn on designs from the history of art, craft and jewellery to inspire the projects. My aim was to create pieces that have their starting point in design movements but are not exact copies of any particular piece of jewellery.

I visited the Victoria and Albert Museum and the British Museum in London; the jewellery collections in both are mouth-watering and I spent many happy hours sketching and studying. I researched jewellery and artistic movements in books and online; there is so much that can be learnt from different sources. You do not have to make complicated drawings or plans for work; simple sketches can remind you of what you have seen.

The book shows different resin techniques that can be adapted by jewellers and craft makers of all disciplines. All the projects use various types of epoxy resin. There are other kinds of resin such as polyester resin, bio resin, UV resin and crystal resin, which will not be used in this book. These projects, however, could be the basis for designs using other types of resins.

Clare John, 2014

Silver-plated Rings 2014 *Silver-plated metal and resin*

1

3

2

4

1 **Ascoli Pendant,** 1976
   Silver and resin.
2 **Dancing Girl Pendant,** 1979
   Silver, 9ct gold, abalone shell and resin.
3 **Dancing Girl Pendant 2,** 1979
   Silver, 9ct gold, titanium and resin.
4 **Tree Earrings,** 1979
   Silver, 9ct gold, abalone shell and resin.

Clare John

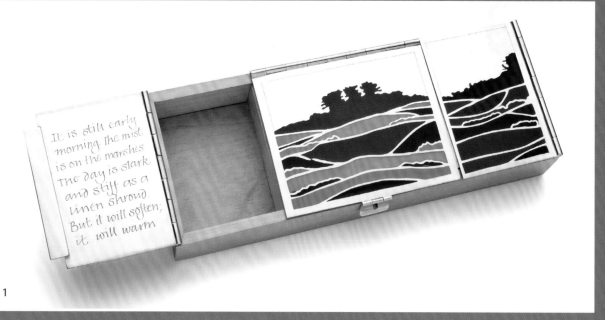

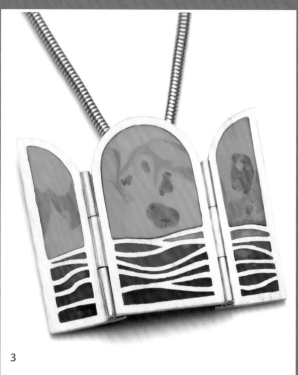

1 **Landscape Jewellery Box,** 1976
   Silver, resin and wood.
2 **Hinged Pendant** (closed), 1982
   Silver and resin.
3 **Hinged Pendant** (open), 1982
   Silver and resin.

Clare John

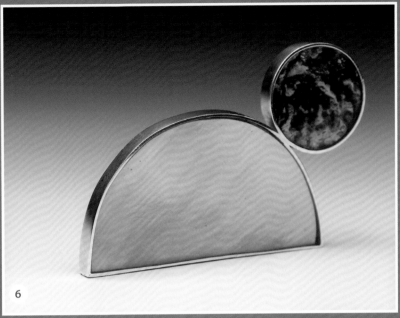

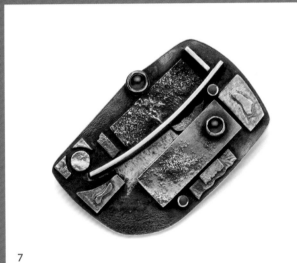

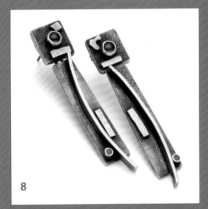

5 Ring, 2011
Silver, titanium and resin.

6 Geometric Brooch, 1987
Silver, mother-of-pearl, abalone shell and resin.

7 Breslau Brooch, 2000
Silver, 9ct gold, garnets and resin.

8 Breslau Earrings, 2000
Silver, 9ct gold, garnets and resin.

7 Mardi gras Rings, 2010
Silver and resin.

Clare John

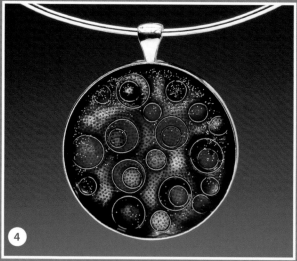

1 Leaf Pendant, 2011
Silver clay and resin.
2 Mosaic Pendant, 2014
Silver-plated pendant, china pieces, beads and resin.
3 Bracelet, 2012
Resin, postcard and silver-plated beads.
4 Pendant, 2012
Silver-plated pendant and resin.
5 Bangle, 2013
Resin and glitter.

Clare John

Materials and Tools

Materials and Tools

Specific resin materials and tools

Resin - low viscosity (enamelling), standard (doming), gel (thixotropic)

Transparent coloured resin

Special effect resin

Pearl and metallic resin

Hardener

Opaque colour pastes

Barrier cream

Digital scales

Plastic mixing cups

Mixing sticks

Cocktail sticks

Kitchen towel

Cotton wool

Nail varnish remover

Tack

Acrylic block 10mm thick in various sizes

Artist's palette knife

Palette paper or a white tile

Everyday tools and materials for resin work

2 part 5 minute epoxy glue

Abrasive polishing cream such as T Cut

All purpose contact glue

Hairspray - an alternative sealer for paper and card

Marker pens

Masking tape

Newspaper or yellow pages

Pens and pencils

Plastic templates

Pointed tool, for example, scriber, pin vice or bead reamer

Protective cover for work surface (for example, plastic tablecloth)

PVA glue

Scissors

Silicone mat

Silicone baking parchment

Sketchbooks

Small flat blade screwdriver

Mould making materials and tools

2 part RTV silicone mould material

Sulphur free plasticene (Plastilene)

Mould box materials such as plastic bottles and cardboard

Large clear plastic cups

Wide blade spatula or palette knife

Sharp knife

Modelling tools

Gaffer tape

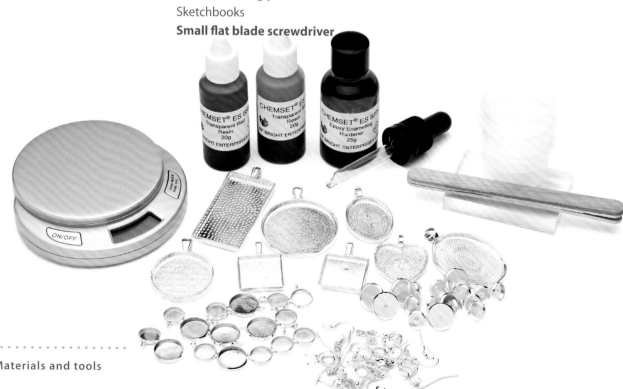

Jewellery tools

Bracelet mandrel
Centre punch
Dividers
Drill bits
Files
Hammers
High-speed drill
Needle files
Oval mandrel
Piercing saw
Pin vice
Pliers
Rawhide mallet
Ring mandrel (also called a triblet)
Saw blades
Scriber
Snips
Steel flat plate
Steel or wood punches
Steel ruler
Steel wool

Soldering equipment

Binding wire
Flux and brush
Plastic tweezers (do not use metal tweezers in safety pickle, they will discolour silver)
Reverse action tweezers (good for holding solder with)
Safety pickle
Solder
Soldering hearth; fire bricks, heat proof mat, charcoal block, soldering wig
Soldering torch
Tweezers in different sizes
Water bowl

Jewellery finishing and polishing equipment

Wet and dry abrasive paper
Buff stick
Barrel polisher (also called a tumble polisher)
Polishing motor
Polishing mops
Polishing compounds; Vonax for plastic, Hi-fin for silver
Micro-mesh polishing cloths

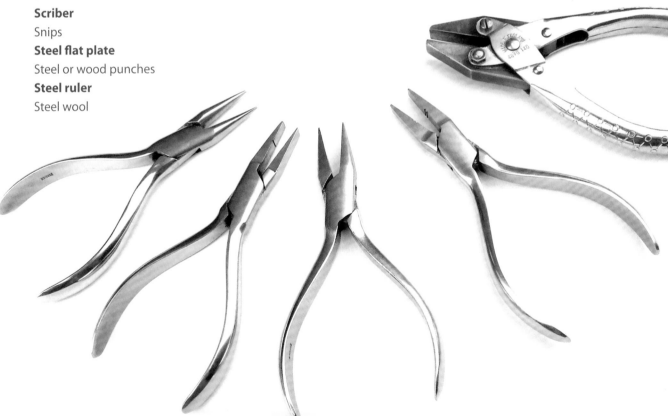

Resins

Three types of epoxy resin are used in this book.
All three can be coloured with colour pastes.

Low Viscosity

resin is a general purpose resin. It comes in clear, transparent, sparkle, pearl and metallic finishes.

Standard

resin is more viscous and is used to form a high dome for a professional finish. It is clear.

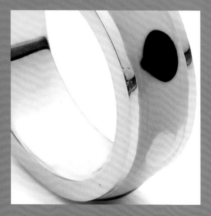

Gel/thixotropic

resin has a thickening agent added to it, so that it is the consistency of thick honey (in contrast to casting or enamelling resin, which are like maple syrup). This means that it is the perfect resin for curved surfaces, such as rings and bangles, where any other resin would drip off.

Basic Resin Instructions

Basic Resin Instructions

When resin and hardener are mixed together, it is magic.
The two liquids mixed together will cure to become a hard, shiny, solid plastic. I love the transformation and the amazing effects you can achieve without lots of equipment and expensive tools.

The following instructions apply to Chemset© epoxy resins. They are measured out by weight:
2 parts resin to 1 part hardener. Other brands will have different measuring ratios. However, these instructions will give you an idea of how all epoxy resins work.

Preparation

Prepare your work area with a protective cover on the surface (which should be level). I use a white plastic tablecloth covered with white paper tablecloths; I throw away the paper cloths when they are too stained. Gather together barrier cream, acrylic block, tack, resin, hardener, digital scales, mixing cups (in different sizes), mixing sticks, cocktail sticks, nail varnish remover, kitchen paper, newspaper and cotton wool. And, last but not least, the piece of jewellery into which you are going to put resin.

Fix the piece of jewellery to the acrylic block by putting tack around the edges, making sure that the mount is level (do not put tack underneath). Do not use too much tack. If the tack goes over the top of the jewellery mount, resin will be pulled over the edge and you will have to clean it off the outside of the jewellery.

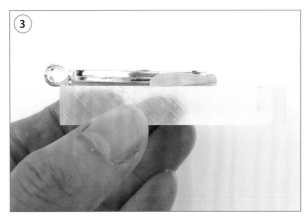

The jewellery must be level with the block. You are going to put liquid resin into it and you do not want it to pool to one side.

Put a pea-sized amount of barrier cream on your hands and rub it in well. If you wash your hands at any time during your work session, remember to put on more barrier cream, before starting work again.

Measuring and mixing clear low viscosity resin and hardener

Resin and hardener come in different containers. Here they are being measured out from tins. You may find it handy to pour resin and hardener into smaller containers so that it is easier to weigh out small amounts. Hardener should always be in a dark glass bottle or tin that stops UV light affecting it; otherwise it can yellow and deteriorate.

Put an empty cup on the digital scales and turn them on (I work in grams so that I can measure out quite small amounts and do not waste resin and hardener). When the scales show 0.0g you can start weighing out resin and hardener because the scales will not now be including the weight of the cup. The cup here is a small reusable plastic cup.

Measure out 2 parts of clear resin; here 2g of resin are being weighed out. I always start with resin because, if you start with hardener, the chemical reaction between resin and hardener will happen more quickly and may give you less time to work.

Add 1g of hardener to the resin in the cup to give a total weight of 3g. Here the hardener is being dispensed using a pipette.

Stir the resin and hardener together with a mixing stick for at least a minute. This is to ensure the two chemicals are properly blended and the chemical reaction takes place. Once mixed, the resin should be usable for about an hour. The time will depend on how warm your workroom is; the warmer it is the shorter the working time. If it is too cold, the mixture will not cure properly. The ideal room temperature is between 18° - 30° C (64° - 86° F).

Tips 1

- The resin mix will gradually change consistency as the curing process happens. I always say that it starts pouring like maple syrup, then thin honey, thick honey, toffee and then it is no longer pourable. It will become hard enough to touch but will still mark when pressed with a fingernail. After 24 hours it will be hard enough to wear.
- Each resin has its own hardener; do not be tempted to use the wrong hardener because this will affect the curing.

Basic Resin Instructions

Adding colour pastes to low viscosity resin

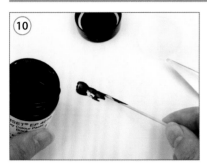

Colour pastes are made from pigment added to a small quantity of resin and will give an opaque colour. You will need a sheet of palette paper or a white tile, cocktail sticks, artist's palette knife, masking tape, kitchen paper, nail varnish remover and cotton wool plus a resin and hardener mix in a cup.
(I advise adding an extra drop of hardener to the resin mix to account for the extra resin in the colour paste). Colour pastes are very intense in colour and you only need a very small amount, so dip a cocktail stick into the paste and put a little bit onto the palette paper or white tile.

Put some resin mix next to the colour paste. Take a tiny amount of paste and add it to the resin mix with the artist's palette knife. Mix the two together so that there are no streaks of colour in the resin (leaving streaks means that the mix won't cure).

Put the coloured resin into the jewellery mount in whatever design you like. Then put a strip of masking tape onto the acrylic block, next to the jewellery and put a drop of resin on the tape. This will be a tester that you can poke with a cocktail stick to let you know when the resin is completely cured/set.

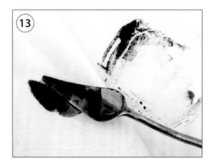

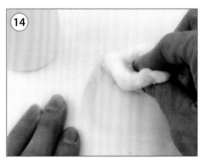

Before it cures, scrape excess resin off the palette paper or white tile onto a piece of kitchen paper or newspaper. Wipe the palette knife with kitchen paper.

Soak some cotton wool with nail varnish remover and wipe the palette paper or white tile clean so that they can be re-used. Clean the palette knife this way too.

Tips 2

- It is a very good idea to label the lids of tins with R for resin and H for hardener. Then the wrong lid will not be put on the tin; I have had lids stuck for all time because I have put a resin lid on a hardener tin.
- If the resin surface of a piece of jewellery becomes scratched over time, you can bring back the shine with another layer of resin. De-grease it with nail varnish remover first.
- Once mixed and cured, resin and hardener will not turn back into liquids.

Mixing other kinds of low viscosity resins

There are many types of pre-coloured epoxy resins. Transparent resin has a dye all the way through it that gives a wonderful translucent colour. It can be made more translucent by adding some clear resin to it. Here I am adding 1g of hardener to 2g of red transparent resin. It is the same ratio of **2 parts resin to 1 part hardener.**

Curing/setting resin

16   Resin should be left to cure in a warm, dust-free place preferably overnight; the ideal temperature is 30° C (86° F). Resin will be hard to the touch in 3 – 4 hours but it will not be fully cured and wearable for 24 hours.

Cleaning tools

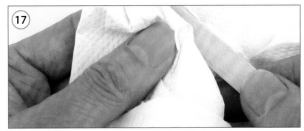

All the resin tools can be cleaned with kitchen paper and cotton wool soaked with nail varnish remover; then they can be re-used several times.

Adding a domed resin layer

When the first layer of resin in a piece of jewellery has cured, you can put on a layer of standard resin. Standard resin looks just like the clear low viscosity resin but it is thicker. This means that it is ideal for building a high dome layer on jewellery. This gives a great professional finish to pieces. The standard resin is also measured out **2 parts resin to 1 part hardener.**
Put a test drop of resin onto some masking tape.

Tips 3

And finally, when wearing resin jewellery...

● Always spray perfume, hairspray and apply cosmetics before you wear resin jewellery. Some of the chemicals we wear can be hard on resin.

Please note that this step ONLY applies to CHEMSET resins, which do not have flammable solvents in them.
As the doming layer is the final layer, it is important not to have air bubbles in the resin, which would spoil the finish. While the resin is still liquid, put the jewellery on the acrylic block onto a heatproof mat. Then pass a gentle flame quickly over the surface; I'm using an oven lighter. The air bubbles will rise to the surface and pop. Do not linger with the flame and do not use this method if there are any flammable items sticking out of the resin surface. (Be careful not to set fire to the masking tape). Once the resin is cured, it is too late to get rid of bubbles.

Basic Resin Instructions

Gel resin (also known as thixotropic resin) has a thickening agent added to it so that it is viscous in contrast to standard or low viscosity resin. This means that it is the perfect resin for curved surfaces, such as rings or bangles, when any other resin would drip off.

The ideal ring has a channel all the way round to protect the resin. Here I am using a ready-made silver ring that is fixed to a mixing stick (you could also use a pencil) with tack.

Push the ring onto the mixing stick with the tack.

Cut 2 'V' shapes into the side of a plastic cup.

The ring, on its mixing stick, sits across the cup inside the 'Vs'. This supports the ring so that it will not fall off the cup. Any resin that might drip off will end up in the bottom of the cup and not on your work surface.

Put an empty mixing cup on the scales and turn them on. Using a mixing stick or palette knife scoop out 1g of gel resin into the cup. It needs to be scooped because the resin is so thick that it will not pour out. This particular gel resin looks yellow in colour but it will set clear.

Add 0.5g of gel hardener. This will give you an ample resin mix for one ring.

Stir the gel resin and hardener mix together. You will notice that the mix will become thinner as you stir. Leave the mix to sit for a minute or so and it will thicken up again.

To colour the resin dip a cocktail stick into some opaque colour paste and put it onto a sheet of palette paper or a white tile.

Put some of the resin mix next to the colour paste and using a palette knife add a tiny amount of the colour paste to the resin mix.

Blend the resin mix and colour paste thoroughly with a palette knife. Make sure there are no streaks of colour paste otherwise the resin will not set.

Put a thin layer of the coloured resin mix into the ring using a cocktail stick. Hold the stick in your hand and turn it (therefore turning the ring) and build up the layer of resin until it is level with the silver ring edging.

Sit the ring back in the 'Vs' of the plastic cup. Keep a close eye on it as the resin may pool at the bottom of the ring. If it does, turn the ring so that the resin levels out. Put a little of the resin mix into the cup as a tester.

Clean all tools with kitchen paper (see page 23).

Health and Safety

It is **extremely** important to follow Health and Safety guidelines when using resin and hardener and making jewellery.

The following guidelines are basic. Visit www.resin8.co.uk for more instructions. You can find specific manufacturers' guidelines on their websites. Detailed jewellery workshop guidelines can be found in books such as 'Complete Metalsmith' by Tim McCreight. There is useful information on The Ganoksin Project website.

Resin and Hardener Guidelines

The chemicals are to be taken seriously and you must look after your own and anyone else's safety when using them.

- Do not let children or pets near the chemicals.
- Store them safely.

The following instructions apply in particular to the Chemset© brand of epoxy resins.

Without protection, the resin and hardener may cause sensitisation of the skin and are harmful if inhaled or swallowed. The hardener can cause severe burns.

- Wear an appropriate barrier cream.
- Work in a well-ventilated room.
- Wear a suitable respiratory mask, if rubbing down with abrasives, and use water to keep down dust.
- Do not eat, drink or smoke while using the resin.
- If chemicals come in contact with skin, wash immediately with plenty of soap and water.
- In case of contact with eyes, rinse immediately and seek medical advice.
- If swallowed, seek medical advice. Do not induce vomiting.

Jewellery Workshop Guidelines

- All soldering, polishing and use of electrical tools should be done with care and thoughtfulness.
- Wear suitable clothing, for example, a cotton apron (tied at the back) or a cotton overall; nylon fabric is flammable.
- Treat all chemicals in a workshop with caution.
- Wear safety goggles and respiratory masks when required; for example, when polishing, soldering, using grinding machines and when using metal filler powders.
- Tie long hair back safely.
- Do not wear open toed shoes in a workshop.
- Do not eat, drink or smoke in a workshop.
- Do not wear loose clothing.
- Do not use machinery without having proper instruction.

RESIN

Projects

Bronze Age Necklace
Casting into ready-made silicone moulds with bronze filled resin

Casting into ready-made silicone moulds with bronze filled resin

Introduction

Bronze is a very useful metal, an alloy of copper and tin; it is much stronger and harder than pure copper. It can be cast into sand and clay moulds as well as being formed with metal working skills. The Bronze Age refers to a period in the history of man between the Stone Age and the Iron Age. The dates vary between countries as to when bronze was first used: from 3000 B.C in Greece and China, and 1900 B.C in Britain. Bronze had many uses including tools, pots, weapons, armour, jewellery and sculpture.

Gold was also used in a lot of jewellery during this time and the necklace in this project is inspired by bronze and gold jewellery. The spiral is a symbol that is ever present in jewellery and has different meanings, for example, infinity in Greek art and growth in Celtic art.

I made this necklace by casting bronze-filled resin into spiral shaped moulds. Because the bronze powder filler is heavier than the resin it sinks to the bottom of the mould and creates a 'skin' of bronze on the surface, which I then polish to look like solid metal. The links are joined together with brass wire findings and jump rings, and hung from braid.

MATERIALS LIST

- Standard resin and hardener
- Black colour paste
- Bronze powder filler
- 2 part 5 minute epoxy glue
- 0.6mm round brass wire x 20cm
- 1.0mm round brass jump rings
- Embroidery threads
- Quick setting contact glue
- Brass catch (I made this clasp using 'Handcrafted Wire Findings' by Denise Peck and Jane Dickerson as inspiration)

TOOLS LIST

- Spiral silicone moulds
- Palette knife
- Palette paper or white tile
- Digital scales
- Mixing cups
- Mixing sticks
- Respiratory mask
- Cocktail sticks
- Pliers – round points, parallel, flat
- Wet and dry abrasive paper
- Fine grade steel wool
- Snips
- 2 small round nails
- Piece of wood
- Hammer
- Acrylic block
- Tack

29

Casting the resin For basic instructions see page 20

In a plastic cup, make a mix of 12g clear base resin and 6g hardener, and add an extra drop of hardener to take into account the black colour paste that will be added. (The colour pastes are pigment mixed with a small amount of resin.) Please note these quantities relate to the moulds shown here and different amounts will be needed for different sized moulds. Take some of the resin mix out of the cup and mix it with some black colour paste on a white tile or sheet of palette paper; mix it thoroughly with a palette knife.

Scoop up the black resin mix, put it back into the plastic cup and stir the clear resin mix until there are no streaks.

Put on a respiratory mask, as bronze powder should not be inhaled. Weigh out 9g of bronze powder and pour it into the black resin mix. Stir the powder into the resin mix.

Put the moulds onto an acrylic block to keep them level and steady. Pour the bronze resin into the moulds. Leave to cure/set preferably overnight in a warm, dust-free place.

Put the moulds into the refrigerator for 30 minutes before releasing the resin from the moulds. This helps the resin come out of the moulds. Bend the moulds carefully to release the castings.

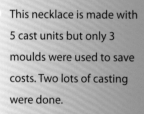

Then give the surface a lovely sheen by rubbing it with very fine steel wool. Cut some steel wool from the packet with scissors. (If you pull it, it will disintegrate)

Rub down the back of the casting on wet and dry abrasive paper; use it wet to keep down the dust and wash the paper when you have finished. Do not rub down much, but enough to give a dull surface over most of the back. This will act as a 'key' for the next layer of resin to stick to. Smooth the sides of the castings on the wet and dry but do not rub away too much.

For full safety guidelines when using bronze powder, visit this page:
www.tiranti.co.uk/EdgeImpactShop/HealthAndSafetyDocs/510-040.pdf?rnd=2014-07-25%2008:52:41

Linking the necklace

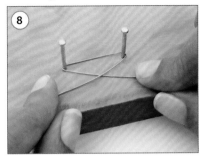

The necklace units are going to be linked by a wire finding with 2 loops, which will be glued to the top of each cast unit. You could drill each unit but this method is neater. Measure across the casting, about 5 or 6mm from the top, which will be the length of the finding that attaches the links together. In this case, the measurement was 30mm. (Do not measure across the middle because the links will tip over and not sit properly when the necklace is worn) Make a jig by hammering 2 small nails, 30mm apart, into a piece of wood. Wrap lengths of 0.6mm round brass wire around the jig. This necklace uses 5 castings so make 5 wire pieces.

Make 4 brass wire findings to fit on each cut end, by turning a loop in the wire and twisting the long end of the wire round the short end.

Fix the finding over the braid and hold with parallel pliers while the long end of the wire is bent round the braid. Pinch it tight with pliers.

Link the braid either side of the castings with brass jump rings.

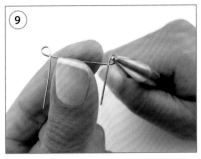

Bend the wire with round pointed pliers to make the 'legs' at right angles to the bar. Tweak them to fit the castings and check that they are all the same size. Flatten them with parallel pliers and snip the 'legs' short.

Make a mix of black resin from 10g clear base resin, 5g hardener (plus an extra drop) mixed with black colour paste, as in Step 1. Cover the back and the wire cross bar with black resin mix; it does not need to be high. Put a test drop of resin mix at the side and leave to cure/set, preferably overnight in a warm, dust-free place.

Attach a clasp on the other end of the braid.

Fix the castings to an acrylic block with a circle of tack, and check that they are level. Glue the finding in place with epoxy glue and leave for 10 minutes to set fully.

Join the castings together with brass jump rings. Make some Kumihimo braid (**Kumihimo braid instructions http://www.youtube.com/ watch?v=2I_uAC_Mxfw [accessed 5 August 2013]**) from suitably coloured embroidery threads to a length that will suit you. Glue at both ends and in the middle with contact glue so it can be cut in half without fraying.

Your necklace is complete.

Peruvian Brooch

Fake resin turquoise inlaid into a handmade brass brooch

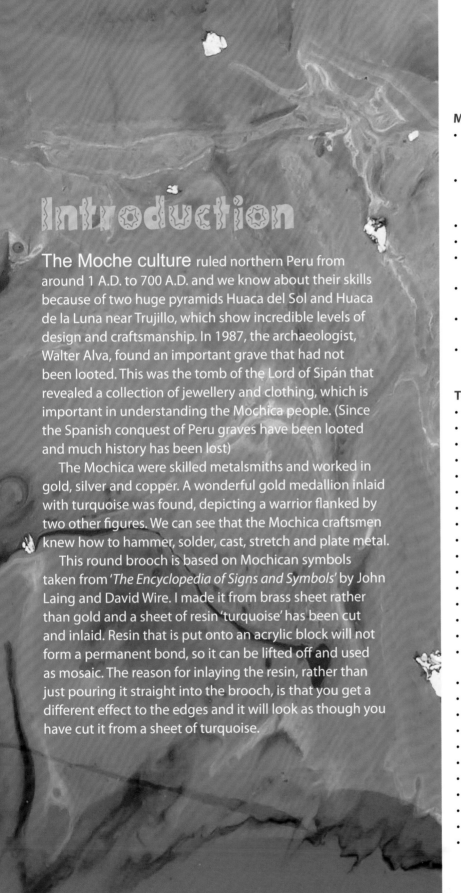

Introduction

The Moche culture ruled northern Peru from around 1 A.D. to 700 A.D. and we know about their skills because of two huge pyramids Huaca del Sol and Huaca de la Luna near Trujillo, which show incredible levels of design and craftsmanship. In 1987, the archaeologist, Walter Alva, found an important grave that had not been looted. This was the tomb of the Lord of Sipán that revealed a collection of jewellery and clothing, which is important in understanding the Mochica people. (Since the Spanish conquest of Peru graves have been looted and much history has been lost)

The Mochica were skilled metalsmiths and worked in gold, silver and copper. A wonderful gold medallion inlaid with turquoise was found, depicting a warrior flanked by two other figures. We can see that the Mochica craftsmen knew how to hammer, solder, cast, stretch and plate metal.

This round brooch is based on Mochican symbols taken from '*The Encyclopedia of Signs and Symbols*' by John Laing and David Wire. I made it from brass sheet rather than gold and a sheet of resin 'turquoise' has been cut and inlaid. Resin that is put onto an acrylic block will not form a permanent bond, so it can be lifted off and used as mosaic. The reason for inlaying the resin, rather than just pouring it straight into the brooch, is that you get a different effect to the edges and it will look as though you have cut it from a sheet of turquoise.

MATERIALS LIST

- Genuine turquoise in any shape or size to use as a colour guide
- Colour pastes; black, white, blue, green gg, regalia blue and yellow
- Clear base resin and hardener
- Gold leaf or gilding flake
- 1mm thick brass sheet 60mm x 60mm
- 0.7mm thick brass sheet 60mm x 60mm
- Hard, easy and extra easy silver solder
- 1.2mm round brass or copper wire 100mm

TOOLS LIST

- Digital scales
- Mixing cups and sticks
- Palette paper or white tile
- Palette knife
- Cocktail sticks
- Acrylic block 100mm x100mm
- Pencil and paper
- Dividers
- Ruler
- Fine blade screwdriver
- Scriber
- Respiratory mask
- Piercing saw and blades
- Files
- Needle files
- Soldering equipment including a soldering wig
- Pliers
- Barrel polisher
- Marker pen
- Snips
- Rawhide hammer
- Steel plate
- Tack
- Abrasive paper
- Wet and dry paper
- Buff stick
- Micro-mesh polishing cloths

33

Making the fake turquoise sheet out of resin For basic instructions see page 20

The starting point is to get some real turquoise and analyse its colour by deciding whether it is a pale turquoise, blue turquoise or green turquoise. Then you choose colour pastes that will make a match. Here I have black, white, blue, regalia blue, yellow and green gg (the brand name of the CHEMSET© colour paste which is very blue/green)

Mix the background turquoise colour on palette paper or a white tile with a palette knife. Then mix some other colours that will make the markings in the turquoise, such as black, dark blue, green and very pale blue.

Make a mix of 12g clear base resin and 6g hardener and add a drop of extra hardener to balance the resin that is in the colour pastes. Add a little resin mix to each colour. Spread a layer of the base turquoise coloured resin onto a large acrylic block. (Do not take it right to the edge because if you do it will be difficult to peel off the sheet when it is set). Use a cocktail stick to add lines and streaks of the other colours through the turquoise. Keep the unused paste to use later in Step 29.

Add some specks of gold leaf. Leave to cure/set in a warm, dust-free place, preferably overnight.

Drawing the brooch design on the brass sheet

Draw out your design. I have used plastic templates here, but you could use a compass or drawing software on a computer.

With a pair of dividers draw a circle 52mm diameter on the 1mm brass sheet. Cut out the circle with a piercing saw.

Tips

- Spare resin can be spread onto an acrylic block to cure. It can be removed and cut up with scissors to make simple mosaic patterns.
- This brooch can be made in other metals such as silver, copper or gold, if you can afford it!
- A smaller brooch could have a brooch pin finding glued to it instead of soldered.

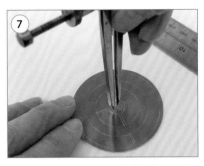

Mark out the design with dividers and scriber.

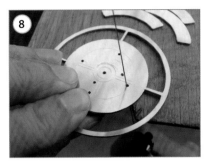

Drill holes and cut out the design.

File the edges of the design.

Cutting the fake turquoise to fit the brass design

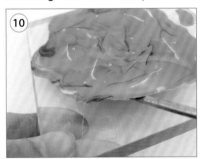

Lift the fake turquoise sheet from the acrylic block by levering it off with a screwdriver.

Look at the fake turquoise and decide which part you want to use in the brooch. Lay the brass onto the fake turquoise and draw through it with a scriber. Do not do this to the areas with a wavy design because this will be very difficult to match exactly and you will fill that area with liquid resin later.

Put on a respiratory mask and cut out the resin with a piercing saw. Keep the saw blade and the resin wet to keep down the dust. When you have finished wash away the dust. Adjust the resin pieces so that they fit in the gaps.

Soldering the brass brooch front to the back

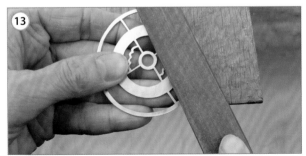

Buff the back of the brass sheet with a buff stick and abrasive paper.

Cut out the 0.7mm brass sheet to fit the brass circle, but do not cut it to the exact size; leave about 1 or 2mm all round. This will make it easier to solder the two pieces together.

Solder the two pieces together with hard silver solder. Solder on a soldering wig so that the heat from the soldering torch will flow round the brass and heat it evenly. Brass is a very dirty metal and you may need to solder a few times. It will have to be pickled and washed in between solderings.

Hammer flat on a steel flat plate. Cut away excess brass from the edge of the brooch. Rub down the back of the brooch with abrasive paper.

Making the brooch pin and catch

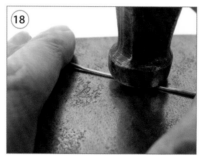

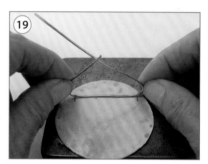

Make the brooch pin and catch out of one length of 1.2mm round copper or brass wire. Cut a 80mm length of 1.2mm copper or brass wire. Lay the wire along the top of the brooch with about 20mm sticking out from the left and 30mm sticking out from the right of the brooch. Mark the wire about 10mm from each side of the brooch.

Hammer the wire flat between the marks with a planishing hammer.

Bend the wire so that the flattened part sits on the back of the brooch.

Solder the wire onto the brooch with extra easy solder.

File the edge of the brooch. File the front of the brooch and buff with abrasive paper.

Hammer the pin with a rawhide mallet on a steel flat plate to harden the wire. Roll the wire as you hammer so that the wire is not flattened.

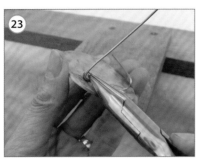

Bend the long side of the wire into a coil around round point pliers to form a short spring.

On the other side of the brooch turn a curve to make the catch and snip it to fit.

Bend the brooch pin over and fit into the catch. Snip the pin to fit and file to a point that will go through fabric.

Test the pin and adjust if necessary. Polish in a barrel polisher.

Fixing the fake turquoise inlay into the brooch

Adjust the inlay to fit. It may need buffing after the soldering because the solder may have taken up some space.

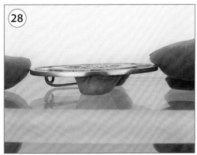

Fix the brooch to an acrylic block with tack. Make sure it is level.

Make a resin mix of 8g resin and 4g hardener with an extra drop of hardener and use the paste left over from Step 3 to match up the colours. Put it into the brooch and glue the inlay into place on top of the resin mix. If the liquid resin comes up at the edges, wipe it away with kitchen paper.

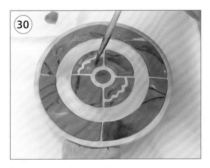

Put some resin into the areas that have the wavy lines and match the extra colours. Put a test of resin mix on some masking tape at the side of the brooch. Leave to cure/set in a warm, dust-free place, preferably overnight. If any resin has leaked over the sides, use Micro-mesh polishing cloths to clean it up.

Alternative version

I made this pendant with mosaic turquoise that I made as in Steps 1-4 and 10, and I cut the fake turquoise up with scissors. I used a ready-made brass pendant with a layer of black resin in the bottom and small mosaic pieces laid in a circular pattern.

MESOPOTAMIAN PENDANT

Imitation cloisonné pendant with glued wire and cold enamel filling

INTRODUCTION

Mesopotamia, which translates as 'land between rivers' included part of Syria, Iraq, Turkey and Iran. It emerged from 5,300 B.C. and lasted into the 7th Century A.D. It is seen by many historians as the cradle of civilisation and was highly sophisticated in areas such as science, mathematics and astronomy. The Mesopotamians invented metalworking, glass and lamp making, textile weaving, flood control, water storage and irrigation.

Early jewellery was made from bronze, gold, silver and electrum (a naturally occuring alloy of gold amd silver with traces of other metals). Stones were imported to add colour to jewellery and enamelling was also used for colour. Men and women wore jewellery, such as earrings, pendants, headbands, ankle bands, signet rings and amulets.

I based the pendant design on a collar in the British Museum, London. It is an enamelled pendant with concentric circles, which are separated by wire borders. This technique is called cloisonné, where wire borders separate areas of coloured enamel. The original has a beaded choker attached.

MATERIALS LIST

- Silver plated round wire 0.8mm x 10cm
- Round silver plated pendant
- Clear resin and hardener
- Blue and white colour paste
- Standard resin and hardener
- Epoxy glue

TOOLS LIST

- Ring mandrel
- Metal snips
- Pliers
- Palette paper or white tile
- Palette knife
- Acrylic block
- Digital scales
- Mixing cups and sticks
- Cocktail sticks

Making and gluing wire circles

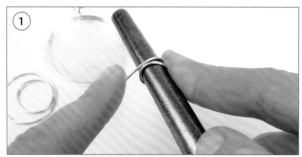

Bend some silver plated wire round a mandrel to make a circle that will fit inside the pendant base.

Snip the wire. Make 2 more circles that will fit inside the 1st circle.

Close the circles with pliers.

Glue the largest circle in place with epoxy glue checking that there are no gaps in the wire, otherwise the colours will bleed into each other.

TIPS

- Use different coloured wires for the circles.
- Bend the wire into any design you like, as long as it does not go over another piece of wire. If it does, it will be impossible to glue the wire flat.

Glue the other 2 circles concentrically in the pendant. Fix the pendant to an acrylic block with tack. Make sure you do not put the tack underneath or over the edges. Check that it is level.

Mixing resin with colour For basic instructions see page 20

Put some blue and white paste onto palette paper or a white tile and mix 4 shades of blue colour. Make a mix of 4gm clear resin and 2gm hardener and add some resin mix to each of the colours. Do not use all the colour mix as it will be too much.

Use a cocktail stick to put each colour into a circle, light colour in the middle going out to the darkest.

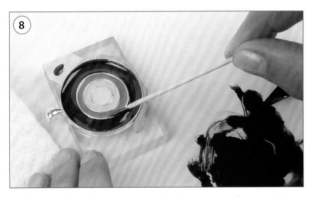

Make sure the colours are completely separate from each other. Put a test drop by the side of the pendant on masking tape. Leave the pendant to cure overnight in a warm, dust-free place.

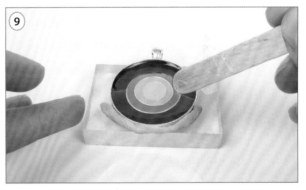

Make a mix of 4gm of standard resin and 2gm hardener for the doming layer. Add a layer over the top of the pendant. Remember to put a test drop of resin next to the pendant on masking tape.

If there are bubbles in the doming resin, put the pendant on the acrylic block on a heat proof mat and pass a gentle flame over the surface. This will draw the bubbles to the surface where they will pop. Do not linger with the flame. Leave the pendant to cure overnight in a warm, dust-free place.

Finish pendant with chain.

Etruscan Agate Necklace

Silver necklace with fake agate resin inlay

3 day advanced project

Silver necklace with fake agate resin inlay

Introduction

This necklace is inspired by an Etruscan piece in the British Museum, London. The original has a row of glass cabochons in gold settings with a textured and granulated edging.

The Etruscans lived in Italy, in a region known as Etruria, which roughly corresponds to modern-day Tuscany. Their culture dates from about the 8th century B.C. until about the 3rd century B.C., after which they were dominated by the Romans. They were extremely sophisticated artists and craftsmen – we know this from the many works that have been found in tombs. Bronze and stone sculpture, pottery, jewellery and painted walls give us a good idea of the skills and culture of the Etruscans. Wealthy women wore long tunics with embroidered hems and colourful mantles or shawls. Necklaces, pendants, earrings, hair ornaments, rings and brooches, made by highly skilled goldsmiths, were worn by the well off.

For this necklace, I made five silver settings and put them on a wire choker. I used resin to make fake agate slices instead of the striped glass. I poured resin directly into the settings so I did not need to make a setting to fit glass cabochons.

MATERIALS LIST

- 1mm square silver wire x 50cm
- Silver sheet 0.7mm x 65mm x 20mm
- Hard silver solder
- 0.8mm round silver wire x 30cm
- Easy silver solder
- Brown transparent resin
- Orange sparkle resin
- Satin white pearl resin
- Hardener
- Standard resin and hardener
- 1.5mm round silver wire x 50cm

TOOLS LIST

- Round metal or wood cylinder x 11mm diameter
- Piercing saw and blades
- Soldering torch
- Soldering hearth
- Soldering wig
- Safety pickle
- Tweezers
- Rawhide mallet
- Oval mandrel
- Files
- 1.5mm diameter round steel wire
- Buff sticks
- Barrel polisher
- Polishing mop
- Digital scales
- Mixing cups and sticks
- Cocktail sticks
- Acrylic block
- Tack
- Pliers

Making the five silver settings

Anneal the square wire so that it is easy to shape. Now bend the wire round a metal cylinder to make a coil of 5 rings.

Cut through the coil with a piercing saw.

Adjust the rings so that the joins fit as tightly as possible.

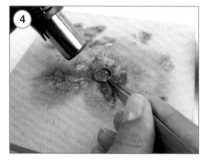

Solder each ring together with hard silver solder. Clean them in safety pickle and rinse in water. Dry them.

Hammer each ring into an oval shape around an oval mandrel using a rawhide mallet. The mallet will not mark the silver as much as a metal hammer.

Using a soldering wig solder each oval onto a piece of silver sheet. Pickle, wash and dry them.

Tips

- If you do not have an oval mandrel, squeeze the circles of wire into an oval shape with pliers. Or make the necklace with round settings.
- Use different colours in the settings.
- Make as many settings as you like but make sure it is an odd number.
- I used silver but I could have made the settings in gold or base metal.

Cut round the edge of the setting.

File the edges of the setting. Also file a flat 2 or 3 mm wide area on the top of each setting.

Alternative version

I used a ready-made silver plated pendant mount and did Steps 12–15. I hung the pendant from a silver plated wire choker.

Making the coil findings for the top of the silver settings

Anneal the 0.8mm round wire, clean and wash it. Make 11 coils of wire at least 6mm long, by wrapping the 0.8mm silver wire round the 1.5mm steel wire eleven times. File the ends of the wire coils to smooth them down.

Solder 1 coil onto the filed flat edge of each setting with easy solder. Pickle and wash them. Polish them in a barrel polisher, which will clean all the silver.

Put a length of binding wire through each coil so that the settings can be held safely. Polish with a polishing motor. Wash in soapy water to remove grease from the polishing compounds. Rinse soap off.

Filling the settings with fake agate slice resin For basic instructions see page 20

Fix all 5 settings onto an acrylic block with tack. Make 3 resin mixes of about 3g each from brown transparent resin, orange sparkle resin and satin white pearl resin. Start by putting a thin edge of brown resin in each setting.

Next put in a thin line of satin white pearl resin.

Then add some orange sparkle resin. Add more resin until an agate effect is achieved. Leave to cure/set in a warm, dust-free place, preferably overnight.

Domed resin layer
For basic instructions see page 20

Put a clear standard resin layer over each setting to add depth to the agate. Leave to cure/set in a warm, dust-free place, preferably overnight.

Putting the settings onto a wire choker

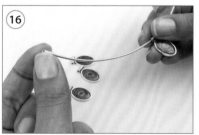

Thread the settings onto 1.5mm round silver wire; alternating them with the six remaining wire coils from Step 9.

The coils act as spacers between the settings.

Work out how long the neck wire should be by trying it round your neck and cut the wire at least 12mm longer to account for the clasp. With pliers bend 2 hooks at the end of the wire, to make a simple clasp. File and buff the ends to make sure they are not sharp or uncomfortable.

Gallery 1

1 **Andrea Coderch** To Be Sexy Or Not To Be Ring, 2011.
Silver and resin. Photo by the artist.

2 **Anna Hall** Amonnite Ring, 2012.
Amonnite, resin and copper with patina finish.
Photo by the artist

3 **Anthea Searle** Paperweight, 2012.
*Silicone mould, resin, watch parts: faces, cogs, hands and
screws.* Photo by the artist.

4 **Antonia Corke** Stamp Necklaces, 2013.
*Original stamps from the 1960s, resin, brass plated
mount and necklace chain.* Photo by the artist.

5

6

7

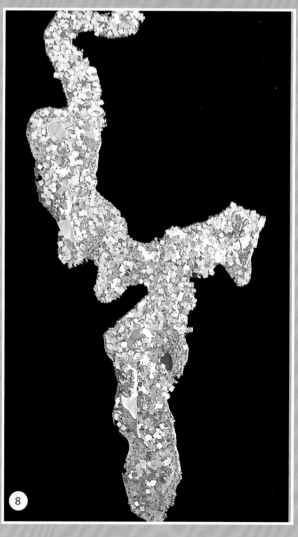

8

5 Carla Nessa Necklace, 2012.
Sterling silver, clear casting resin, resin pigments and soft artist pastels.
6 Carla Nessa Jello Shot Rings, 2011.
Sterling silver, clear casting resin, resin pigments and soft artist pastels.
7 Carla Nessa Earrings, 2012.
Sterling silver, clear casting resin, resin pigments and soft artist pastels.
Photos by Guy Nichol.
8 Francesca Marcenaro Lava Light Resin Necklace, 2012.
Resin, glass mirror, silver and pyrite.
Photo by Keith Leighton.

Gallery 1

1 **Dawn Gear** Constellation Earrings, 2012.
   *Sterling silver, resin, gold wire, gold leaf, leaf skeleton
   and Japanese seed beads.*
2 **Dawn Gear** Constellation Earrings, 2012.
   *Sterling silver, resin, gold wire, gold leaf, leaf skeleton
   and Japanese seed beads.*
   Photos by the artist.
3 **Gemma Goodall** Red Button Bangle, 2013.
   Resin and buttons.
4 **Gemma Goodall** Autumn Leaf Button Bangle, 2013.
   Resin and buttons.
   Photos by the artist.

5 **Erica Rowan** Snake Skin Mokume Pendant (Scar Formations), 2013.
Copper, mokume (copper & brass), shed snake skin, resin and white acrylic paint.

6 **Erica Rowan** Snake Tail Pendant (Kaa's Progression), 2011.
Copper, shed snake skin, resin and white acrylic paint.

7 **Erica Rowan** Snake Skin Ring (Perpetual), 2011.
Copper, shed snake skin, resin and white acrylic paint.

8 **Erica Rowan** Paint Chip Pendant (What Lyle left behind), 2011. *Copper, bronze, rusted red paint chip, resin and black enamel paint.*
Photos by Ron Regan (Regan Photography).

Elizabethan Necklace

**Silver flowers painted with gel resin,
silver knots and pearl links**

2 day advanced project

Silver flowers painted with gel resin, silver knots and pearl links

MATERIALS LIST

- 1mm silver sheet 30 x 40mm
- 0.8mm round silver wire x 70cm
- Easy silver solder
- Gel resin
- Hardener
- White pearl mica powder
- Red violet colour paste
- 0.2mm round silver wire x 130cm
- 64 white freshwater rice pearls x 7.5mm
- 16 pale blue freshwater rice pearls x 7.5mm
- 0.8mm silver wire jump rings x 32

TOOLS LIST

- Tracing paper
- Pencil and paper
- All purpose glue such as Bostik (UK) or Tombow (USA)
- Piercing saw and blades
- Needle files
- Barrel polisher
- Pliers
- Snips
- Buff stick
- Abrasive paper
- Soldering equipment
- Safety pickle
- Tweezers
- Acrylic block 10 x 10cm
- Silicone non slip matting
- Masking tape
- Digital scales
- Mixing cups
- Cocktail sticks
- Palette paper or white tile
- Palette knife
- Pin vice
- 0.8mm drill bit
- Dremel or similar high-speed drill

Introduction

It is very rare to find whole, undamaged inexpensive jewellery from the past. Even today, as tastes change, most jewellery is melted down to make more fashionable pieces. Only heirlooms in museums have been saved from this fate. Cheaper jewellery is lighter and less durable than more expensive pieces, so it was immensely valuable to find, in 1912, a collection of everyday jewellery, from the early 1600s. It is called the Cheapside Hoard and can be seen in the Victoria and Albert Museum and the Museum of London. I was inspired by that collection to make this necklace, which includes lots of chains with flowers, knots, pearls and enamel.

Imagine a woman in a velvet gown with brocade decoration with a long pearl necklace. Queen Elizabeth I was a lover of pearls and managed to inherit a wonderful collection of pearl necklaces when she had Mary Queen of Scots beheaded.

Making the silver flowers

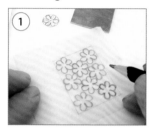
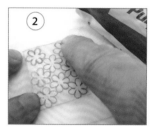
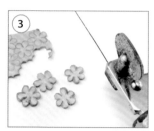

Draw a circle 10mm in diameter. Divide into 6 equal segments and draw into 6 petals to make a flower. Draw a rectangle 30 x 40mm on tracing paper and trace the flower 8 times inside the rectangle.

Glue the tracing paper drawing onto the 30 x 40 mm silver sheet with an all-purpose glue. Do not use an epoxy glue or super glue, as they will make the paper stick too firmly to the silver sheet. Leave to dry.

Cut out the flowers with a piercing saw.

Peel off the tracing paper and file the edges with a needle file; you can even up the flowers if you need to. Buff both sides of the flowers to remove any traces of glue and rough edges. Polish in a barrel polisher.

Making the silver knots from wire, while the flowers are in the barrel polisher

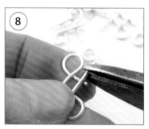

Wrap 0.8mm round silver wire around a 4.5mm needle file handle or a nail, so that you have two 'legs' at right angles. Snip each 'leg' to a length of 10mm. Make 16 of these. Adjust them with pliers so that the cross over meets snugly.

Solder the join with easy solder then pickle and wash them clean.

Position one silver wire piece on top of another to create a knot. You are aiming for a diamond shape between the two loops. You may need to tweak with pliers so that they sit tightly. Solder both joins where the 'legs' cross over, with easy silver solder. Pickle and wash clean.

Snip off the 'legs' leaving about 2mm on both sides to form a little cross.

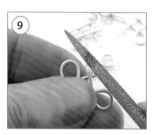

Clean off the sharp edges with a needle file and a buff stick or abrasive paper. Thread all the knots onto a length of scrap wire and tie it up as this will make it easier to fish them out of the barrel polisher. Polish in a barrel polisher for about 30 minutes.

 Tips

- Substitute garnet or amethyst beads for some of the pearls.
- Put a resin coat on the reverse of the flowers to have a double-sided flower.
- Make a pair of drop earrings from the knots and flowers.
- Make a ring from a larger flower soldered to a ring shank.

Putting gel resin on the flowers For basic instructions see page 20

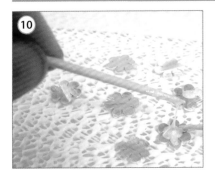

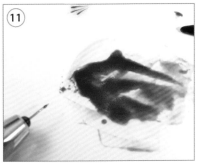

Wash and buff one side of the flowers to give a 'key' for the resin to stick to. Cut non-slip silicone matting to fit the acrylic block and fix onto the block with masking tape. (This is so that the flowers will not slip and slide) Lay the flowers buffed side up on the silicone matting. Measure out 1g of gel resin and 0.5g of hardener in a small mixing cup and blend thoroughly. Put half of the resin mix onto the palette paper or white tile and add some pearl mica powder. Mix with a palette knife. Coat each flower with a layer of pearl resin using 2 cocktail sticks so you can hold the flower in place with one and coat with the other.

Put the rest of the resin mix on the paper or tile and add a speck of red violet colour paste and mix completely with the palette knife. Practice drawing red violet through some of the leftover pearl resin with a pin (held in a pin vice for comfort).

Draw lines on the pearl with the red violet resin using the pin. Put a dab of resin mix on the masking tape as a tester. Leave the flowers to cure/set in a warm, dust-free place, preferably overnight.

Assembling the necklace

Use a pin vice with a drill bit, to make location holes on 2 opposite petals of each flower. (This will prevent your high-speed drill from skidding on the resin surface) Using a 0.8mm drill bit drill all the way through with a Dremel or similar tool.

With round pointed pliers, bend 0.2mm silver wire into a loop and wrap the wire round to make a wrapped loop at one end. Thread on 2 white pearls, 1 blue pearl and 2 white pearls and make another wrapped loop at the other end. Make 16 of these.

Use jump rings to attach a flower at one end and a knot at the other end of each pearl section until you have a continuous necklace, which is long enough to put over your head.

A version of this project first appeared in issue 53 of 'Making Jewellery' magazine

17ᵗʰ Century Cloisonné Pendant

Silver soldered cloisonné pendant with cold enamel resin

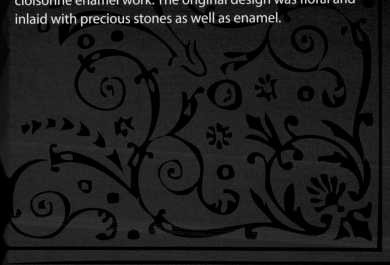

Introduction

Cloisonné is a very old technique that involves making borders in metalwork and filling the enclosed areas with either vitreous (glass) enamel or cut stones. (Cloisons means 'partitions' in French) This technique has ben used by many cultures from the Ancient Egyptian, Roman, Byzantine, Chinese, and Visigoth and it is still used today.

In traditional enamelled jewellery very thin wires are glued with gum tragacanth (a natural glue) to a base made of metal. Powdered glass is then put in the little fields and fired into place, in a kiln. (The wires are like pencil lines in a drawing). In this pendant I have soldered silver wire in place. Without a barrier such as the wire, it is difficult to stop colours bleeding into each other.

17th Century English jewellery (before the Puritans came into power) was elaborate and highly decorated. I based this pendant on a locket, which was covered in delicate and ornate cloisonné enamel work. The original design was floral and inlaid with precious stones as well as enamel.

MATERIALS LIST

- 1mm silver sheet 50mm x 50mm
- 0.8mm round silver wire 20cm
- Hard and easy silver solder
- Blue transparent resin
- Satin white pearl resin
- Red sparkle resin
- Green transparent resin
- Blue sparkle resin
- Hardener

TOOLS LIST

- Tools
- Scriber
- Piercing saw and blades
- Oval template sheet
- Pliers
- Ring mandrel or punch
- Soldering equipment
- Soldering wig
- Planishing hammer
- Steel block
- Barrel polisher
- Polishing motor and mops
- Polishing compounds
- Digital scales
- Small mixing cups
- Mixing sticks
- Cocktail sticks

55

Designing and preparing the silver pendant for soldering

Draw variations of the design and select one to use.

Draw round an oval template onto silver sheet with a scriber. Cut round the shape with a piercing saw to make a silver oval.

Bend a gentle curve in the 0.8mm silver wire using any curved surface, for example this ring mandrel.

Check the curve of the wire against your drawing of the petals. Snip off about 10cm of the curved wire, which will make 8 petals. Put the wire on the drawing of a petal and mark at the point of the petal with a marker pen.

Cut partway through the wire where you have marked the point of the petal, with a piercing saw. DO NOT cut all the way through.

Carefully bend the wire with the part cut section acting as a hinge. Cut partway through the hinge and bend again. Do this until the wire bends into the petal shape that you want. Alternatively you could file a groove with a triangular needle file to score the hinge.

Soldering the wire to the pendant

Cut the wire to fit the drawing and make 8 petal shapes. Make 7 jump rings by wrapping silver wire round a needle file handle and sawing them. Close the jump rings tight.

Solder the petal shapes first at the hinged end and then at the open end with hard solder. Solder a jump ring for the middle of the flower.

Make sure the silver oval is grease free. Solder the petals and jump ring onto the silver oval with hard silver solder. Do it one by one so that you get the positioning right.

Making the wire spirals

Bend a curve in 0.8mm round silver wire with round point pliers.

Snip off the little straight bit of wire at the beginning of the curve. This will give you a nice tight curve on the spiral.

Turn up a spiral. Make 3 more.

Solder the spirals and jump rings in place

Mark and cut the spirals to fit between the petals. Solder in place with hard silver solder. Pickle, wash and dry thoroughly.

Hammer the pendant flat with a planishing hammer on a steel plate. Buff the sides of the pendant with a buff stick.

Solder 3 small jump rings together as shown and then solder 2 of them to the top of the pendant. Put a large jump ring through the top small jump ring and solder it closed with easy silver solder. Pickle, wash and dry.

Polishing the pendant

Buff the back of the pendant. Barrel polish the pendant and then polish it on a polishing motor. Wash it very thoroughly afterwards to make sure there is no grease left anywhere.

Adding resin to the pendant
For basic instructions see page 20

Fix the pendant to an acrylic block with tack and make sure it is level. Mix the first resin colour, 2g satin white pearl resin and 1g hardener, and fill in the little circles. Then mix 2g transparent blue resin with 1g hardener and add some of the satin white pearl mix to it. This will give a solidity and sheen to the transparent blue. Fill the petals with blue/white resin mix using a cocktail stick. Take care that you do not get any blue in the white circles. Do not forget to put a test drop of resin mix at the side on some masking tape. Leave to cure/set in a warm, dust-free place.

When the blue and white resins are hard, make a mix of 2g red sparkle resin with 1g hardener and fill in either side of the pendant. Put a test drop on the tape and leave to cure/set in a warm, dust-free place.

When the red sparkle resin is hard, make two mixes of 2g green transparent resin with 1g hardener and 2g blue sparkle resin with 1g hardener. Finish the pendant with these two colours. Put a test drop on the tape and leave to cure/set in a warm, dust-free place, preferably overnight.

Alternative version

Use a ready-made pendant and glue in shaped wires to make the 'cloisons'. The trick is to make sure the wire is glued properly so that the resin colours do not leak into the next compartment. The wire should be glued with 2 part epoxy resin glue which is compatible with the epoxy resin.

Tips

- Allowing different colours of resin to cure or partially cure before adding another colour stops colours bleeding into each other.
- The pendant could have the resin added after being barrel polished and Step 16 could be missed out - it would just be less shiny.
- The surface tension of the resin means that it does not pour over the edge of the pendant.

Mourning Ring

Silver ring inlaid with gel resin

Introduction

Jewellery so often tells a story. It is handed down through generations, worn to display wealth and fashion, and it can be commissioned to mark an event. Rings are given for engagements and weddings; although not popular now, for many centuries the bereaved had jewellery made to remind them of the loved one. The Victoria and Albert Museum has a fine collection of mourning rings, one of which was the inspiration for this ring. The original has a pattern bearing engraved names and dates and is beautifully enamelled in white, black and a dove grey/blue.

I have simplified the design and the resin colours evoke the original enamels. The resin used is different from low viscosity or standard resin; it is thixotropic or gel resin because a normal resin would simply drip off a curved surface. Gel resin is perfect for rings and domed surfaces because its viscosity means it does not pour off. However there is a disadvantage to the thickness of gel resin as it is not easy to eliminate bubbles and most pieces have to have bubble holes filled, if the resin is rubbed down and polished. Persevere because it is a wonderful material.

I used a ready-made sterling silver ring with a channel, to which I added a decorative silver band or you could make the ring from scratch.

MATERIALS LIST

- Silver ring with a channel
- Silver sheet:
  1mm x 70mm x 10mm
- Hard silver solder
- Gel (thixotropic) resin and hardener
- White, black, regalia blue colour pastes

TOOLS LIST

- Needle files
- Binding wire
- Ruler
- Pair of dividers
- Piercing saw and blades
- Curved template or coin
- Centre punch
- High-speed drill
- Round nose pliers
- Soldering equipment
- Ring mandrel
- Rawhide mallet
- Buff stick with abrasive paper
- Barrel polisher
- Mixing stick or pencil
- Tack
- Plastic cups
- Scissors
- Digital scales
- Mixing cups
- Palette paper or white tile
- Palette knife
- Broken saw blade
- Respiratory mask
- Polishing motor
- Calico mop
- Inside ring felt mop
- Vonax polishing compound

Making the decorative band

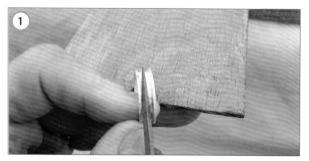

File the channel in the ring to make it ready to solder a decorative band.

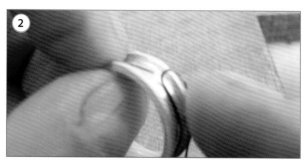

Use the binding wire, to determine the circumference of the ring inside the channel.

When you measure out your length of wire, you have to take into account the curving of the decorative band. To do this, add 1½ times the thickness of the silver sheet to the circumferance of the channel. In this case, the silver sheet is 1mm thick so add 1.5mm.

Measure the width of the inner channel with a pair of dividers. Then close the dividers by about 0.5mm so that the decorative band will not touch the edges of the channel (see inset picture).

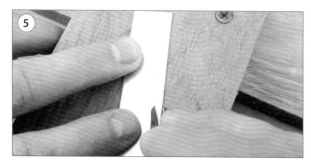

Mark a strip of silver to the length and width of the channel. Cut out the strip; this will be the decorative band.

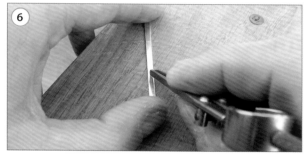

Use the dividers to mark down the centre of the strip by setting them to half the width of the silver strip.

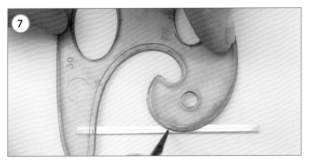

Divide the strip evenly into 6 and find a curved template (it could be a coin) and draw 6 curves on each side to give a scalloped look.

Cut out the scallops and file them to make sure they are even.

Use the dividers to mark a thin border on each side of the scallops.

Mark each section with a centre punch and drill holes through the decorative band; you should have 6 holes.

Pierce out the middle of the scallops ensuring that there is enough silver between each section to leave a strong link. If you cut away too much there is a danger the silver will break when you bend it round the ring.

File the scallops with a needle file so that they look neat and even.

Tips

- The gel resin could be filled in to just below the surface of the silver and left as it is without being cut back and polished.

  The resin would not be flush with the silver.

- Gel resin is useful for putting on domed surfaces as well as rings and bangles.

- Rings and bangles that are filled with gel resin need a border or edge – otherwise the resin can chip when it is knocked.

  Rings are the most vulnerable items of jewellery as they get the most wear and tear.

Shaping the decorative band to fit the silver ring

13

Bend your band gently in the middle with round nose pliers.

14

Fit the curve of the band to the ring.

15

Solder the middle of the band to the channel with hard silver solder. Do not try to solder it all in one go because it is too difficult. Pickle, wash and dry. Then bend the band round the rest of the ring. Adjust it if necessary by filing at the join. Wrap binding wire around the band (to hold it in place while soldering) and finish soldering the strip with easy silver solder. Remove binding wire before pickling, washing and drying.

Cleaning the ring for the resin inlay

16

Hammer with a rawhide mallet to level the band and flatten it down.

17

File and buff the ring with an abrasive paper. Polish in a barrel polisher and wash all soap off it, so that it is not greasy.

Alternative version

I made a version of the ring using the silver ring without a decorative band soldered in. The dove grey/blue resin has had circles of black and white resin added in 8 evenly spaced spots, by using a cocktail stick, while the grey/blue resin was still liquid. The circles are not exactly the same but they are close enough. The grey/blue resin could also be drilled when it is set and the other colours put into the drill holes to create the design.

Preparing the ring for the resin inlay For basic instructions see page 20

Fix the ring onto some tack wrapped round a mixing stick or pencil to make a 'spit' that can be turned. This will enable you to complete one colour at a time. Cut 2 V shapes out of a plastic cup and sit the ring on its 'spit' across the cup. The V shapes will mean that the 'spit' and ring will not slide off the cup and you can turn it, if the resin pools at the bottom.

Make a resin mix of 1g gel resin and 0.5g hardener in a small mixing cup. Add white colour paste to it on palette paper or a white tile. Put the white resin mix into alternate sections of the decorative band and slightly overfill so that the resin is proud of the silver. You can use a cocktail stick but a broken piercing saw blade is an excellent tool. The resin does not slide off it and you can put tiny amounts into corners. Leave the resin to set/cure in a warm, dust-free place, preferably overnight. Do not be tempted to put the other colours of resin in until the first one is set. If you accidentally drip one of the other colours into the white, you will have to clean it out and start again. Do not forget to put a test spot of resin mix on masking tape.

When the white resin is set, make another mix of 1g gel resin and 0.5g hardener and add some black colour paste that has had a tiny amount of regalia blue paste added to tone down the black. Put this resin into the remaining sections of the decorative band. Leave the resin to set/cure in a warm, dust-free place, preferably overnight.

Make a colour mix of white, regalia blue and a tiny speck of black to create a dove grey/blue. Make a third resin mix of 1g resin and 0.5g hardener. Blend the colour on palette paper or white tile with a palette knife. Keep some of the colour paste mix to one side in case you need to fill any holes later. (This is so that you can get the same colour match). Fill in the main part of the ring and leave to set/cure in a warm, dust-free place, preferably overnight.

Finishing the ring

Wearing a respiratory mask, buff away the excess resin using wet and dry paper, on a buff stick that is wet. Wash the buff stick afterwards. You will probably find holes in the resin where there were air bubbles. If so, fill them with more resin and leave to set/cure and buff again.

Polish the ring on a polishing motor using a plastics' polishing compound such as Vonax. It is easier to hold a ring to a polishing mop if you put the ring onto an inside ring felt; your fingers do not get hot holding the ring.

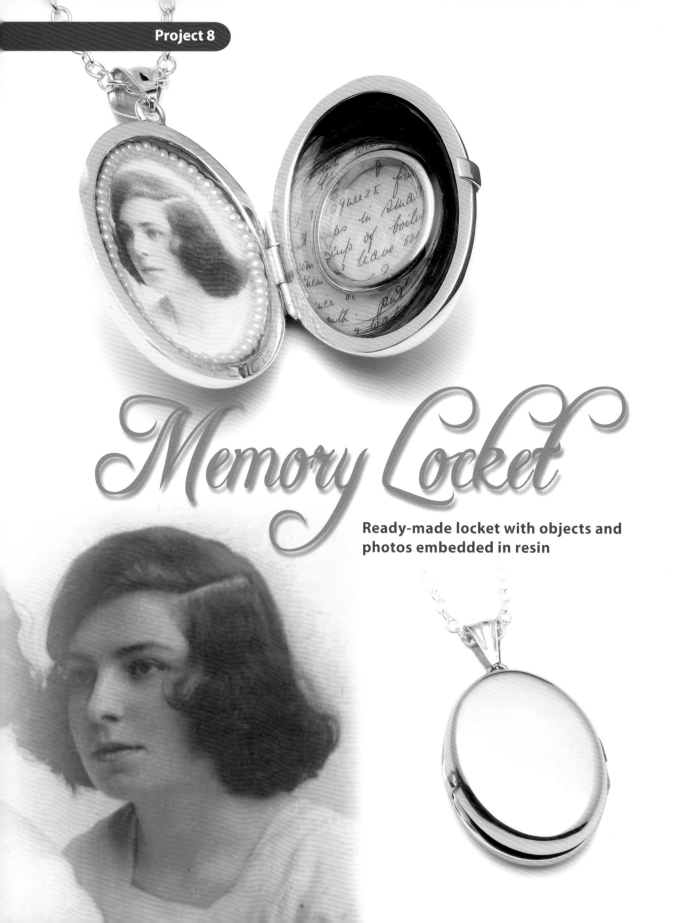

Memory Locket

Ready-made locket with objects and photos embedded in resin

Ready-made locket with objects and photos embedded in resin

Introduction

This project is a locket that combines things that have important memories for me. It is in memory of my grandmother, Anita, and includes a photo of her as a young woman, a lock of her hair, her wedding ring, some of her handwriting and some tiny pearl beads. She had beautiful handwriting that did not change throughout her life and I have included a copy of her recipe for marmalade, that I use every year. I have used a ready-made silver locket for the piece and embedded or set the items in resin. You can include any items that have a meaning for you but they need to be dry, as any moisture will make the resin cloudy and affect the curing/setting.

MATERIALS LIST

- Ready-made locket
- Photos on high quality photo paper
- PVA glue
- Low viscosity resin and hardener
- Small pearl beads
- Sewing cotton
- Epoxy glue
- Mementoes such as lock of hair, wedding ring, handwritten text, fabric, buttons, broken jewellery, dried flowers, anything that will fit in the locket
- Acetate sheet suitable for your printer
- Satin white pearl resin and hardener

TOOLS LIST

- Scissors
- Paintbrush
- Digital scales
- Mixing cups
- Mixing sticks
- Cocktail sticks
- Acrylic block
- Tack
- Computer, scanner and printer

Locket and jewellery © Trustees of the British Museum

65

Preparing the photo and fixing it inside the locket For basic instructions see page 20

Find a suitable photograph, scan it and size it to fit the locket. I have used a programme on the computer (Microsoft Word) to crop it to an oval with a border. Print it out on high quality photo paper. Cut to fit the locket. Seal the photo twice on each side by painting it with PVA glue using a brush. Make sure the glue is bone dry before you use the photograph in the locket.

Fix the locket onto an acrylic block with tack and make sure it is level. It is best to use the tack in an oval ring shape, as it is easier to balance the locket that way. The photo is going to be on the base of the locket.

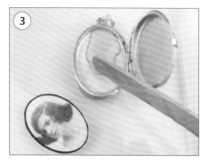

Make a mix of 2g low viscosity resin with 1g hardener and put a thin layer in the bottom of the locket. Press the photo into the resin mix which will glue it in place.

Take care that there are no air pockets under the photo by pushing it down and put a thin layer of resin over the top.

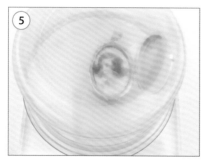

Cover the piece to prevent dust getting into the resin and leave to cure/set in a warm, dust-free place, preferably overnight. Do not put the piece into a curing cabinet or on a source of heat; if you do, you will get bubbles in the resin, as air will come out of the paper.

 Tips

- You could use photos on both sides of the locket.
- Check that everything fits and that the locket will close before you fix the items in place with resin and glue.
- Test any hair in resin before you start the piece, to see if it will look good.

Second resin layer inside the back of the locket For basic instructions see page 20

Thread the pearl beads on some sewing cotton and fit a border round the edge of the photo. Threading them means that all the beads are evenly spaced and you do not see the holes in the beads. Knot the thread and snip close so there are no loose threads. Use epoxy glue to glue the pearls neatly to the edge of the locket. Make sure the beads are not too high and do not affect the closing of the locket.

Make another mix of low viscosity resin and seal everything in place but do not make it a deep layer. Leave to cure/set in a warm, dust-free place, preferably overnight.

Preparing the text for inside the front of the locket

Scan a handwritten piece of text and size it to suit the locket. Then print it on acetate sheet on a computer printer. This means that you will see the text but not the medium it is printed on. Cut a suitable part of the text to fit the locket.

Satin white resin layer in the other half of the locket

Fix the locket to the acrylic block so that the other half of the locket is now level. Make a mix of 4g satin white pearl resin and 2g hardener. This is not a flat white colour and will give texture to the back. Put a thin layer of white resin mix in the base of the locket – about 1 to 1.5mm deep. Leave to cure/set in a warm, dust-free place, preferably overnight.

Fixing the text, lock of hair and wedding ring into the locket

Make a mix of 4g low viscosity resin and 2g hardener. Put a thin layer of resin mix on top of the white pearl and push the text into place. The resin mix is acting as glue.

Put more of the resin mix on top of the text and put some of the lock of hair in place. You can use a cocktail stick to move it to where you want it to be.

Put the wedding ring in last and adjust the position of things. Leave to cure/set in a warm, dust-free place, preferably overnight.

Gallery 2

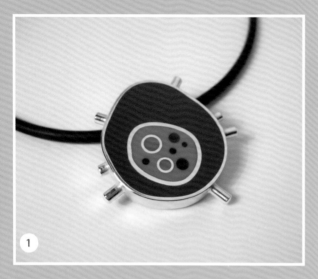

1 **Islay Spalding** Biomorph Pendant on Rubber, 2009.
  Silver and resin.
2 **Islay Spalding** Biomorph Ring, 2012.
  Silver and resin.
3 **Islay Spalding** Biopools Necklace, 2008.
  Silver, paper and resin.
4 **Islay Spalding** Biomorph Rings, 2005.
  Silver and resin.
  Photos by the artist.

5

6

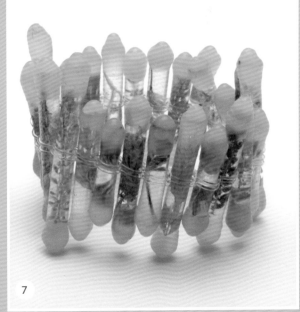

7

5 **Erika Uzmann** Salt Shakers, 2011.
   Resin, chalk and silver.
6 **Erika Uzmann** Plant Matter Bracelet, 2009.
   Resin, dye, brass and monofilament.
7 **Erika Uzmann** Buoy Bracelet, 2009.
   Resin, plants, wax and stretch cord.
   Photos by the artist.

Gallery 2

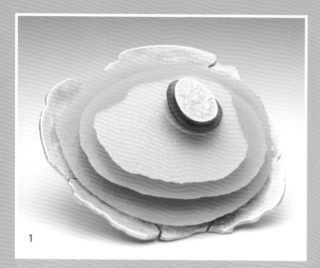

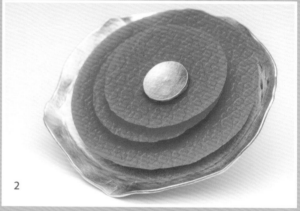

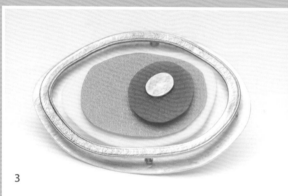

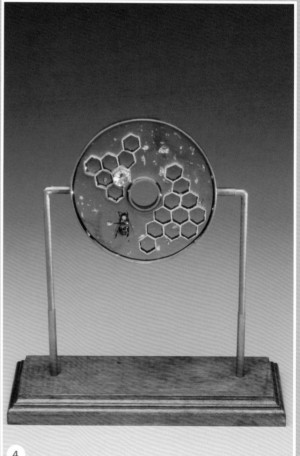

1 **France Roy** Pink Lady, 2011.
   Sterling silver, resin, pigments and rivet.
2 **France Roy** Rose Again, 2013.
   Sterling silver, resin, pigments and rivet.
3 **France Roy** Urban Sunset, 2013.
   Sterling silver, resin, pigments and rivet.
   Photos by Anthony McLean.
4 **Wei Lah Poh** Cellective Reproduction, 2011.
   Silver, resin and dry pigments. Photo by the artist.

5 **James Thurman** Layered Synergy, 2012.
*Thurmanite® (recycled maps & epoxy resin) Damascus
steel, sterling silver and findings.*
6 **James Thurman** Layered Synergy, 2012.
*Thurmanite® (recycled maps & epoxy resin) Damascus
steel, sterling silver and findings.*
7 **James Thurman** Thurmanite® Twig Pin collection, 2013.
Thurmanite® (recycled paper & epoxy resin) and findings.
Photos by the artist.

Art Nouveau
Plique-à-jour Earrings

Transparent resin in silver earrings

Transparent resin in
silver earrings

Introduction

Art Nouveau is the exuberant style that developed after William Morris' Arts and Crafts Movement in the 1890s and is seen as the bridge between heavy Victorian aesthetics and the Modernism of the early 20th century. Art Nouveau artists used flowing lines and images taken from nature. Lilies, daffodils, ivy, tulips, daisies, dragonflies, bees, grasses and so on appeared in anything from buildings to glassware, clothing and jewellery.

Plique-à-jour means 'letting in daylight' - these earrings do not have a backing and look like stained glass. The technique is usually a vitreous/hot enamelling process and was developed in the 6th Century during the Byzantine Empire. It was revived by 19th century jewellers, like René Lalique, who became interested in making jewellery for the design rather than the intrinsic value of the pieces; many of them used materials not seen before in precious jewellery such as moulded glass and horn.

I designed this project to show how to use resin, without a backing, to achieve the stained glass effect. This tecnique is not practical for large areas because there is a danger that the resin could be pushed out of its setting.

Daffodil image © www.crimsoncirclestudios.com.au

MATERIALS LIST

- Tracing paper
- Contact glue such as Bostik (UK) or Tombow (USA)
- Silver sheet: 1.5mm x 30mm x 45mm
- 0.8mm round silver wire x 200mm
- Easy silver solder
- Yellow, green and blue transparent resin
- Hardener

TOOLS LIST

- Piercing saw and blades
- Parallel pliers
- Dividers
- Centre punch
- Drill and 0.8mm drill bit
- Soldering equipment and torch
- Metal snips
- Files
- Needle files
- Buff stick – abrasive paper 240 grit
- Barrel polisher
- Polishing motor
- Polishing compounds
- Acrylic block – new
- Plasticene
- Digital scales
- Mixing cups and sticks
- Gas lighter
- Flathead screwdriver (not a Philips)
- 10mm round punch - metal or wood
- Round nose pliers

Transparent resins

Designing the silver earrings

Draw ideas based on a plant or flower. The leaves of a lily plant were the starting point for these earrings. The shapes are curved and fluid.

Decide which shape to use and sketch ideas for the ear wires on tracing paper on top of the leaf to visualise the final design. The ear wire must have 2 points of contact with the earring.

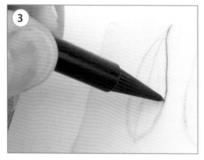

Scan the leaf drawing and resize to about 36mm long. Copy it in a mirror image and print up the two images. Make copies onto tracing paper.

Spread contact glue on the back of the tracing and onto the silver sheet. Leave to dry for a few minutes and then press firmly together.

Cutting out the earrings

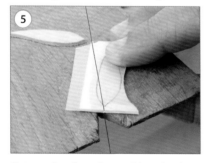

Cut out the silver sheet with a piercing saw.

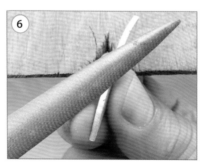

File the edges.

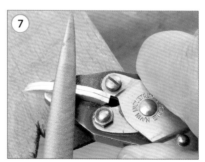

Clamp both earrings together in parallel pliers and file so that they match.

Set a pair of dividers to 1mm wide and mark a line all the way round each earring.

Mark each earring with a centre punch and drill a hole at least 0.8mm wide.

Pierce out the inside of each earring.

File the inside with a needle file.

Cutting and soldering wire on the earrings

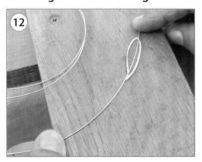

Lay the 0.8mm silver wire on top of each earring and cut a length about 50mm longer than the top of the earring.

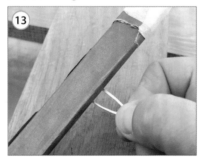

Buff one side of each earring, making sure it is the opposite side of the second earring.

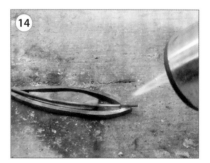

Lay an earring, buff side up, on a soldering mat and put the offcut of silver sheet in the middle; this is to support the silver wire during soldering. Place the wire over the earring. Paint flux onto the wire and earring where they meet. Solder the wire at the top and bottom with easy solder. When both are soldered, pickle and wash the earrings.

Finishing the earrings before putting the resin in

File the outside edge of the earrings so that they have soft curved edges. Snip and file the end of the wire at the bottom of the earrings. Buff and polish in a barrel polisher.

Polish the earrings on a polishing motor. Wash them to remove all polishing compound, so that they are grease-free.

Preparing to put the resin in

Put the earrings flat side down onto a new acrylic block. Seal the edges with plasticene so that resin cannot leak out.

Turn over the acrylic block and check the seal on the back.

Adding transparent resin to the earrings For basic instructions see page 20

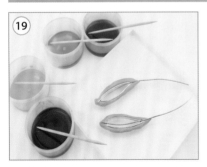

Mix 3 colours of transparent resin – here we are using yellow, green and blue for the leaves. 2g resin to 1g hardener will be plenty of each colour. Mix some green and yellow together to give you a fourth colour.

Put the resin into the earrings with a cocktail stick or similar fine tool. Do not put a thick layer in but do make sure it goes up to the level of the wire; this will help secure the resin. Swirl the colours so that they blend a little.

Put a tester of the resin colours at the side on some masking tape. Pass a gentle flame quickly over the surface to make air bubbles rise and pop. Leave to cure/set in a warm, dust-free place, preferably overnight.

Completing the earrings

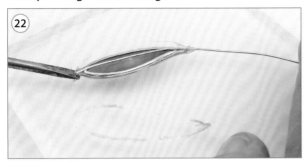

When the resin is set, gently lever the earrings off the acrylic block. The resin will appear to be stuck to the acrylic block but it is not a permanent bond and will lift off.

Carefully scrape off any resin that might have seeped onto the silver. If the silver becomes scratched, it can be polished again with polishing cloths or on a soft piece of leather impregnated with polishing compound.

Bend the long wires at the top of the earrings round a 10mm diameter punch or wooden form. Shape the wires with round nose pliers to give a smooth curve.

Buff the end of the wires to take off any sharp edges.

Tips

- Use any fluid shape from nature as the starting point of the design.
- Use ready-made metal frames.
- Resin does not stick to silicone or other 'greasy' surfaces but it is easier to fix the earrings and seal the edges on an acrylic block. The acrylic needs to be new otherwise it might not be flat and scratch free.

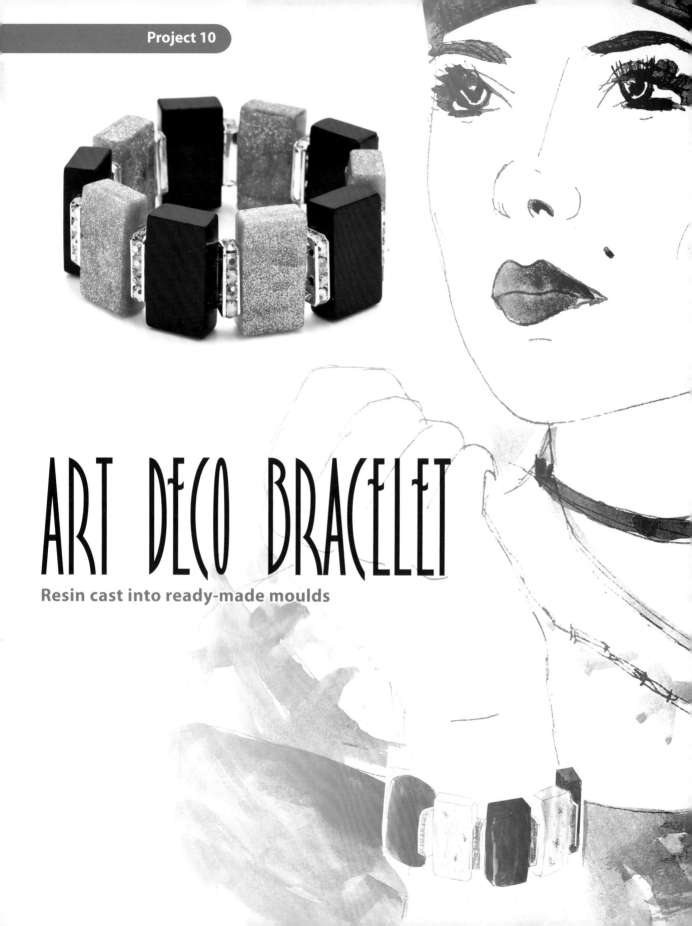

ART DECO BRACELET

Resin cast into ready-made moulds

INTRODUCTION

Art Deco is the name given to the modern style of art and decoration that started in France in the 1920s and spread worldwide. It is recognisable by its use of geometric shapes, symmetry, clean lines and rich ornamentation. It died out before the Second World War but has been revived and re-used many times.

Art Deco embraced modern technology and the materials of its time. Architecture used geometric shapes and flat, white concrete, while jewellery was made from both expensive materials such as platinum and diamonds and from inexpensive materials such as the new synthetic plastic Bakelite (which was invented by Leo Baekeland in 1903). This bracelet is inspired by Bakelite designs and by a visit to the Chrysler building in New York.

In the first bracelet I made, I drilled holes all the way through the resin castings, to turn them into beads that could be strung on elastic. However, the bracelet in this project has plastic tubing embedded in the middle to avoid the task of drilling.

Illustration © Stephanie Beever 2013

MATERIALS LIST
- Low viscosity resin and hardener
- Black colour paste
- Silver glitter resin
- Clear plastic tubing 4mm thick
- Plasticene
- 2 part 5 minute epoxy glue
- Standard resin and hardener
- Clear beading elastic
- 10 spacer beads
- Contact glue with needle applicator

TOOLS LIST
- Rectangular silicone chocolate mould
- Acrylic block 10cm x 10cm
- Mixing cups
- Mixing sticks
- Digital scales
- Palette knife
- White tile or palette paper
- Scissors
- Dividers
- Respiratory mask
- Piercing saw and blades
- Pointed tool (to remove the plasticene)
- Non slip silicone matting
- Wet and dry abrasive paper 280 grit
- Micro-mesh polishing cloths or abrasive polishing cream such as T Cut

These instructions are for a medium sized bracelet.

Casting the first two resin mixes For basic instructions see page 20

Make a mix of 16g low viscosity resin and 8g hardener in a plastic cup. Put a small amount of black colour paste onto a white tile or palette paper. Add some of the resin mix and blend thoroughly with a palette knife. Put this black mix back into the plastic cup and stir until there are no streaks. It should be a solid opaque black colour.

Put the chocolate mould onto an acrylic block to keep it firm and level. Pour some black resin mix into two compartments to about 3mm deep.

Make a mix of 16g silver glitter resin and 8g hardener and pour into 2 other compartments of the mould to the same depth of 3mm. Leave the resins to cure/set in a warm, dust-free place, preferably overnight, until they are hard.

Setting the plastic tubing into the moulds

Cut lengths of plastic tubing to fit the longer side of the rectangle mould, 2 for each compartment.

Seal both ends of the tubing with plasticene so that resin will not get in.

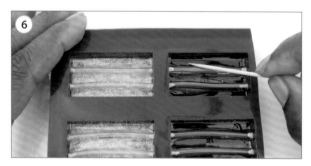

Using 2 part epoxy glue stick the tubing at equal distances apart, on top of the resin. Leave the glue to set hard.

Make 2 more resin mixes as in Steps 1 and 3. Cover the silver glitter resin with more silver glitter and the black resin with more black resin. Check that the tubing is covered. Leave to cure/set in a warm, dust-free place, preferably overnight.

De-moulding the castings and cutting the castings into beads

8

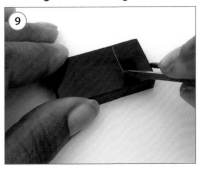

9

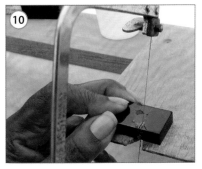

10

Put the moulds into the refrigerator for 30 minutes, then gently open up the moulds and take out the castings. The part that was at the bottom of the mould becomes the top of the bead.

Each casting will make three beads so set your dividers to a third of the length of the casting, 16mm in this case. Then mark each casting into thirds.

Wear a respiratory mask for this step. Cut through along the marked line with a piercing saw to make rectangular beads. Keep the saw blade wet to contain the dust. Rinse the resin bead frequently to wash off the dust and wash the work area when you have finished.

Putting the final coat of resin on the back   For basic instructions see page 20

11

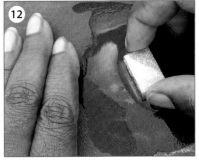

12

13

Clean the plasticene out of the tubing.

Wear a respiratory mask for this step. Rub down the back of each bead to remove the raised edge, with wet and dry abrasive paper that is wet. Keep it wet to contain the dust.

Put some non-slip silicone matting on the acrylic block and put the resin beads with the tops facing down (so the face that has just been rubbed down is now uppermost). To bring back the shine and make the backs of the beads smooth and comfortable to wear, make a mix of 10g standard resin and 5g hardener. Put a layer on each bead to cover the back. Put a test drop of resin mix beside the beads. Leave to cure/set in a warm, dust-free place, preferably overnight.

Finishing the beads for threading on elastic

Rub down the corners and any sharp edges with Micro-mesh polishing cloths. Polish the sides of the beads with the polishing cloths too. Alternatively you can polish the sides with an abrasive cream.

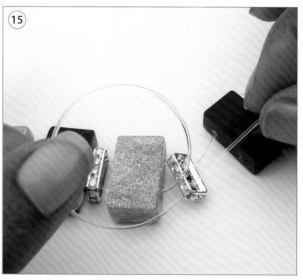

Thread the beads with diamanté spacer beads on beading elastic. Alternate your black and silver glitter beads.

Sparkle Resins

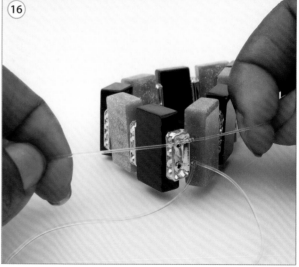

Pull the elastic thread very, very tight and knot the elastic.

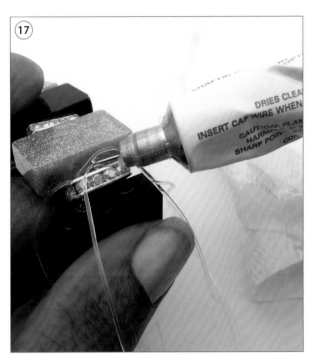

Seal the knot with some contact glue or clear nail varnish.

Your bracelet is ready to wear.

TIPS

- Any shape mould could be used to make beads - it will need to be deep enough to be able to sandwich the tubing between 2 layers of resin.
- The mould needs to have a shiny surface so that the casting will be shiny.
- The beads could be polished on a polishing mop with Vonax polishing compound.
- The rectangular beads could be angled on the sides where they meet so that the bracelet does not have gaps at the joins.

DOUBLE-SIDED AFRICAN NECKLACE

Resin used in borderless units

INTRODUCTION

This necklace was inspired by African jewellery pieces made from coloured discs and coins. Jewellers all over the world have upcycled unlikely materials in their designs; items that one culture will regard as of no value will be seen by others as interesting and precious. This necklace is double-sided for two reasons: it gives a choice of colours and also the resin on the reverse stops the copper discs tarnishing skin or clothing. I wanted to show how resin stays on a flat, borderless surface without going over the edges, due to the resin's viscosity.

© Tropenmuseum of the Royal Tropical Institute (KIT)

MATERIALS LIST

- 14mm diameter copper blanks x 30
- Small coins x 9
- White pearl resin
- Hardener
- Red, green and yellow colour pastes
- Standard resin
- Black, white and red oxide colour pastes 30gm jars
- Silver plated wire 0.8mm round or ready-made jump rings
- Leather cord
- Silver plated necklace fastener to fit on the cord

TOOLS LIST

- Buff stick and abrasive paper
- Silicone mat
- Acrylic block 10cm x 10cm
- Digital scales
- Mixing cups
- Mixing sticks
- Palette knife
- Palette paper or white tile
- Cocktail sticks
- Kitchen paper
- Drill bit in pin vice
- High-speed drill
- 0.8mm round drill bit
- Pliers

85

Prepare the copper for the resin process

Buff both sides of 30 copper blanks to remove any grease and give a textured surface for resin to stick to.

Line up the copper blanks on a silicone mat placed on the acrylic block. This will stop them sliding all over the place.

Colour Pastes

First resin coating For basic instructions see page 20

Make a mix of 4g of white pearl resin and 2g of hardener. Add an extra drop of hardener to account for the resin in the colour pastes.

Use red, green and yellow colour pastes to add to the white pearl resin mix.

TIPS

- This could be made as a one-sided necklace with only one colour range - seal the back with varnish or wax to slow down tarnishing.
- It can be made without the coins.
- Make drop earrings to match the necklace.

Put a small amount (on the tip of a cocktail stick) of each colour paste onto palette paper or a white tile. Add about ¼ teaspoon of white pearl mix to a speck of paste and mix thoroughly with a palette knife. Clean the knife well, with kitchen paper, between colours.

Put red resin mix on 14 copper blanks, green resin mix on 10 copper blanks and yellow resin mix on the remaining 6. Add drops of differing colours in the middle of the blanks, if you like, to create variety. Put a tester of resin on the silicone mat. Leave to cure/set in a warm, dust-free place, preferably overnight.

Second resin coating For basic instructions see page 20

Check the resin is cured by poking the tester with a cocktail stick. When it is cured, turn the blanks over.

Make a mix of 4g clear standard resin and 2g hardener. Add an extra drop of hardener. Put a small amount of resin mix on palette paper and add some red oxide paste. Do the same with black and white colour paste.

Put white resin mix on 19 blanks, black resin mix on 6 blanks and red oxide on 5. Put a tester of resin on the silicone mat. Leave the resin to cure in a warm, dust-free place, preferably overnight.

Linking the necklace together

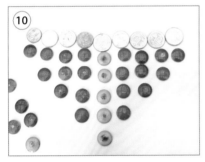

When the resin is completely cured, lay 25 blanks out in a design that you like, making sure that the reverse will look good too. There will be too many blanks, but that is to make sure that any that might be faulty can be discarded.

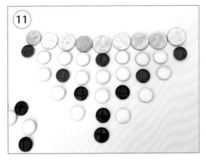

This is the reverse of the necklace. Work out where the blanks will need to be drilled to link up to each other. Some will need 1 hole and the rest will need 2 holes.

Mark links with a location drill by hand. Then drill through with a high-speed drill using 0.8mm drill bit. Drill the coins too - they will all need 3 holes. Some coins will be very hard to drill; the easiest ones are US one cent pieces.

Make 35 jump rings from 0.8mm wire and use them to link the blanks together.

Link the coins along the top of the necklace.

Add a leather cord (to a length that suits you) with fastener, to each side of the necklace.

1960s Fluorescent Ring
Tailor-made silicone mould with resin casting

Introduction

The 1960s was a time of radical change in fashion and jewellery design. New materials were being developed and bright, jazzy colours were used. Mary Quant introduced the mini skirt and Courrèges pioneered the space age look in fashion. Jewellery was chunky and big pieces were made from block coloured plastic. It was a time for throwing out the concept of expensive jewellery in precious materials and bringing in 'groovy' new styles.

I designed this Fluorescent Ring to show the spirit of the 1960s when bold colours and modern plastics were used in fashion. I made it using a ready-made ring as a master, making a silicone mould of the ready-made ring and casting fluorescent coloured resin in layers to create stripes.

The fluorescent resin glows under UV light!

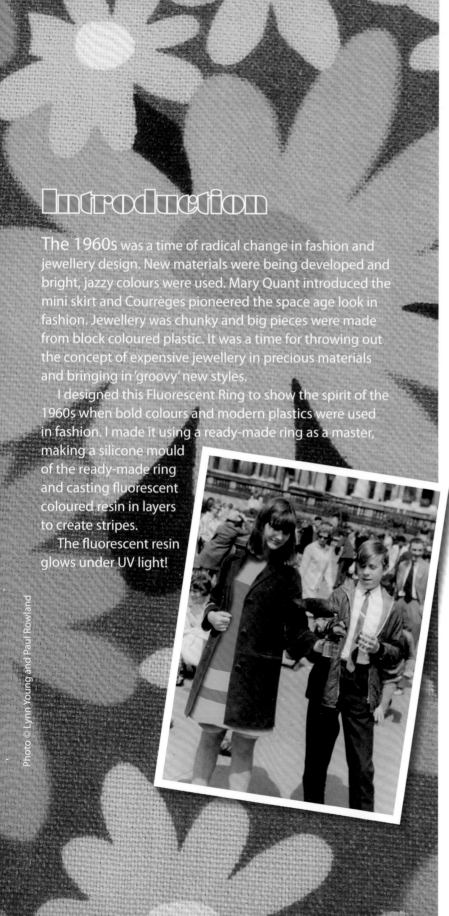

Photo © Lynn Young and Paul Rowland

MATERIALS LIST

- Plastic master ring – it is important to have a flat side that can be attached to the base
- Mould box e.g. shampoo bottle
- Plastilene – a sulphur free plasticene (sulphur interferes with the curing of silicone)
- Rice
- Silicone mould material
- Resin and hardener
- Fluorescent pink and yellow colour paste
- White colour paste

TOOLS LIST

- Saw
- Modelling tool
- Gaffer tape
- Marker pen
- Clear plastic cups
- Scales
- Wide blade sticks or palette knife
- Brush
- Drinking straw
- Palette knife
- Palette paper or white tile
- Mixing cups
- Mixing sticks
- Airtight pots
- Respiratory mask
- Wet and dry abrasive paper 180 grit
- Buff stick
- Micro-mesh polishing cloths 1500 to 12000 grit
- Polishing paste such as T Cut (optional)

89

Making a mould box for the ring

Find a plastic shampoo bottle or similar that the ring will fit into with at least a 10mm space all round it. This will be the mould box.

Mark the bottle into 3 sections – the top that has the lid section, the middle, which is a tube and the bottom which has a base. The middle and the bottom pieces must be at least twice the height of the master ring. Cut into the three sections and discard the top part.

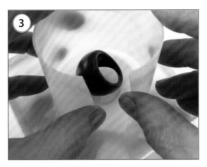

Cut the section of the bottle that is a tube along its length so that the tube will open.

Fixing the ring master inside the mould box

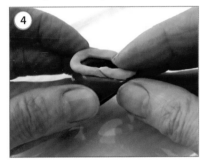

Put some Plastilene (sulpher-free plasticene) around one side of the ring.

Fix the ring with the Plastilene to the acrylic block.

Clean the edge of the Plastilene so that there is a neat edge around the ring.

Wipe the master ring so that there are no streaks of Plastilene or other marks on it.

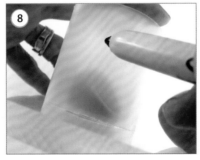

Hold the tube over the ring against the acrylic block and mark it at least 15mm above the height of the master ring. This will be the level to which the silicone mould material is poured. The tube will be fixed around the ring later.

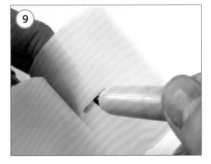

Mark the same level onto the other part of the bottle, which had the base left on it.

Measuring and mixing the silicone

Pour some rice into the bottle base up to the mark. Transfer the rice to a clear plastic cup. This will give you the total volume of silicone that you will need to make the mould. The silicone material comes in 2 equal parts so mark the clear cup approximately half way up and that will give the level for 1 part of the silicone.

Empty the rice out of the cup and brush the cup out to make sure there is no rice dust left inside. Put the cup on the scales, turn them on and pour in 1 part of the silicone up to the halfway mark on the cup; in this case it is blue. You should use a clear cup so that you can see the level that the silicone has reached. Make a note of the weight of the 1st part of silicone.

Put another cup on the scales and turn them on. Measure out the same weight of the 2nd part of the silicone material (white). Only then pour the white into the cup with the blue. (Do not pour the white onto the blue when weighing it out. Because, if you add too much, you will not be able to rectify it by removing any as it will already be mixing with the blue).

Fold the two colours together with a wide bladed stick or palette knife. Do not stir vigorously as this would introduce more air into the mix, which is not good. Pour the mix back into the other cup and this will make sure that every bit of silicone is mixed properly. (The advantage of 2 colours of silicone mould material is that it is easy to see when the material is mixed evenly throughout)

Tips

- Always have separate tools for resin and silicone work, otherwise you will find the ingredients of one will affect the other and alter the curing of both.
- Warming the mould makes the resin flow more evenly into the mould.
- Drill holes in the ring and fill them with a different colour resin to make a spotty ring.

Pouring the silicone into the mould box

(14) Paint a thin layer of silicone mix onto the master ring with a brush. This will break the surface tension on the ring and make sure it is coated all over with silicone.

(15) Take a drinking straw and blow gently on any visible bubbles; they will pop and disappear. Do not blow too much as this will blow moisture from the breath onto the silicone and that will inhibit the silicone curing/setting.

(16) Seal the inside of the open side of the tube with gaffer tape. Fix the tube around the ring onto the acrylic block with a little gaffer tape to locate it. Then seal very thoroughly with Plastilene all round.

(17) Turn the acrylic over and check that the seal is good. This is essential because the silicone mould material will leak at every opportunity and, once it leaks, it is difficult to seal as everything will be slippery with silicone!

(18) Pour the silicone mix into the mould box. Do not pour it directly onto the master but into the area around it. This is so as not to disturb the thin layer that was painted on and to avoid bubbles. Try and pour a thin steady stream of silicone from as high as possible. The thinner the stream the fewer bubbles there will be in the mould.

(19) Fill the mould box to the marked line that you made in step 8. Once the master is covered you cannot see how deep the mould needs to be which is why you have the pen line. Leave the silicone to cure/set for 24 hours in a warm place.

(20) Remove the outside Plastilene seal.

(21) Peel away the mould box. It will lift off the acrylic very easily.

(22) Gently lift out the master from the mould. Leave the mould to post cure/set for 3 hours in a warm place.

First resin layer in mould For basic instructions see page 20

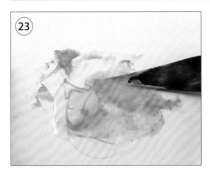

(23) Mix some fluorescent pink colour paste with a speck of white colour paste on palette paper or a white tile. Make a mix of 4g of resin and 2g hardener and add an extra drop of hardener to make up for the colour paste that will be added. Mix a small amount of colour paste (do not use all the colour paste) into the resin mix using a palette knife; make sure it is mixed completely with no streaks of colour paste.

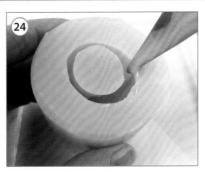

(24) Leave the resin to sit so that bubbles can escape. Put the mould above a radiator or in a very low oven, with the door open, for 20 minutes. Warming the mould helps the resin flow. Put some of the resin mix into the mould. Do not put too much as this is the first stripe. The aim is to fill it one third full.

(25) Tilt the mould so that the resin flows around it evenly. Put a drop of resin mix at the side of the mould so that the curing rate can be tested.

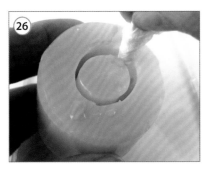

(26) Wrap a bit of kitchen paper on a cocktail stick and wipe any drips of colour off the walls of the mould.

(27) Put the mould on an acrylic block, tilt it and put a wedge under it so that the resin will cure/set at an angle. Leave the mould in a warm, dust-free place, preferably overnight.

(28) Reserve some of the colour paste mix in an airtight pot to use for the third resin stripe. This is not the resin mix, but the colour paste that you made in step 23.

Alternative version

I used a ready-made ring mount and added pink and yellow resin in concentric circles.

Second resin mix For basic instructions see page 20

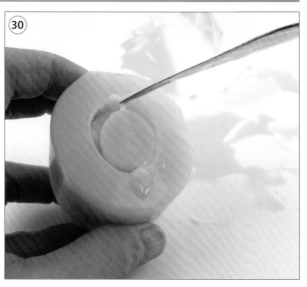

Make a mix of fluorescent yellow and a speck of white colour paste. Weigh out 4g of resin and 2g of hardener with an extra drop of hardener. As before, mix a small amount of colour paste with resin mix on palette paper or a white tile. Blend completely. Leave to sit for 10 minutes or so for bubbles to escape.

Warm the mould and put some of the resin mix into the mould, tilting as before to spread the resin. Clean the sides of the mould with kitchen paper.

Fluorescent Colour Pastes

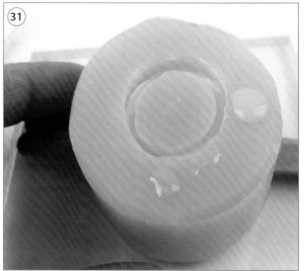

Leave the resin to cure/set tilted on sticks or a wedge but not at the same angle as for the pink layer. Put a drop of resin as a tester on the side of the mould. Let it cure/set in a warm, dust-free place, preferably overnight.

Third resin mix For basic instructions see page 20

(32)

Make a third mix of 4g resin and 2g hardener with an extra drop of hardener. Add some of the reserved pink colour paste to the resin mix. Again leave your resin to sit for 10 minutes. Warm the mould as in step 24.

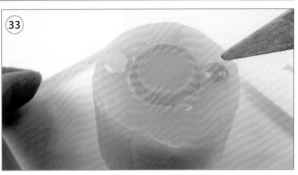

(33)

Fill the warm mould to the top with the third layer of resin mix. Do not forget to put a tester drop on the side of the mould. Leave to cure/set in a warm, dust-free place, preferably overnight.

(34)

Test the sample drop of resin to make sure it is really hard. Put the mould in the refrigerator for 30 minutes before peeling apart the mould and gently removing the cast ring.

(35)

Wear a respiratory mask to avoid breathing resin dust. Clean up the edge of the ring with a buff stick covered in wet and dry abrasive paper. Use it wet and wash afterwards. The resin is quite easy to rub down.

(36)

Clean and polish the ring with Micro-mesh polishing cloths. It is worth taking time to go through from coarse to very fine grades of cloth.

(37)

The ring could be polished on a buffing machine but, as the resin is fairly soft and the ring has a complex shape, it is easier to polish by hand. It can also be brought to a soft shine using an abrasive paste such as T Cut.

A version of this project first appeared in issue 55 of 'Making Jewellery' magazine

Gallery 3

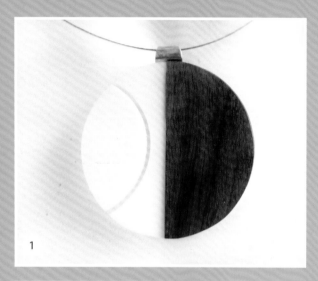

1

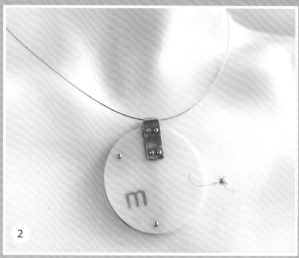

2

3

1 **Melissa Osgood** Resin and Wood Pendant (front), 2012.
   Laser cut acrylic, resin, wood and silver.
2 **Melissa Osgood** Resin and Wood Pendant (back), 2012.
   Laser cut acrylic, resin, wood and silver.
   Photos by the artist
3 **Lynn Durie** On the Green Cufflinks, 2011.
   Silver, resin and oil paint. Photo by Gordon Sutton.
4 **Nicole Iredale** Caterpillar Ring, 2011.
   Resin. Photo by the artist.

4

5 **Kristyn Cooper** Picture Books, 2011.
   Silver, paper and resin.
6 **Kristyn Cooper** Halloween, 2011.
   Silver, paper and resin.
7 **Kristyn Cooper** Peaceful, 2011.
   Silver, paper and resin.
   Photos by Jeff Crawford.

Gallery 3

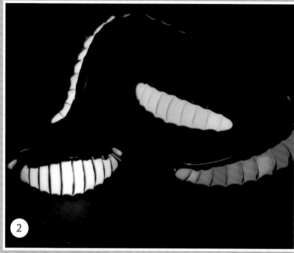

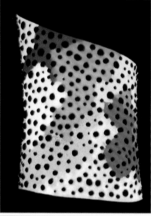

1 **Tyra-Jane Ward** Body Slug, 2012.
   Silver, resin and glow-in-the-dark pigments.
2 **Tyra-Jane Ward** Body Slug, 2012.
   Silver, resin and glow-in-the-dark pigments.
3 **Tyra-Jane Ward** Body Slug, 2012.
   Silver, resin and glow-in-the-dark pigments.
   Photos by the artist.
4 **Sadie Blythin** Paper Rings, 2012.
   Paper and resin. Photo by the artist.

5

6

7

5 **Jane Dzisiewski** Assorted Resin Stones, 2012.
   Sintered metal, polyester resin, pigments.
6 **Jane Dzisiewski** Bangles, 2010.
   Sintered metal, polyester resin, pigments.
7 **Jane Dzisiewski** Pendant with resin stone
   mounted in sterling silver and 9ct gold, 2012.
   Sintered metal, polyester resin, pigments,
   sterling silver, 9ct gold.
   Photos by the artist.

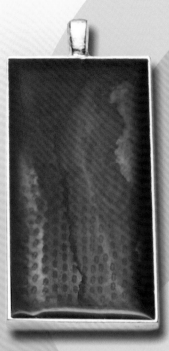

1970s
Birth of Studio Jewellery

Resin mixed with pigments in ready-made pendants

Introduction

The 1970s saw a flowering of the studio jewellery movement. Jewellery was made professionally by designers who had not been trained through the conventional apprenticeship route. Art Schools began to develop diplomas in modern jewellery design, led by teachers and makers such as Gerda Flöckinger.

When I went to Art School in the 1970s, I was encouraged by a tutor to explore resin and I have been using it in my work ever since. The materials were very strong smelling and unpredictable, and a lot of work was needed to bring the resin surface up to a good shine. The resin would cure with a sticky surface, which had to be rubbed down and then polished with a polishing motor. The colour pigments were rudimentary and I used artist's oil paints to colour the resin. This sometimes made the surface have a 'wormed' effect; a kind of streaking that can be avoided by using just a tiny amount of paint or the modern colour pastes which are tailor-made for colouring resin.

I have recreated the kinds of pieces I made in the 1970s with modern resin coloured with oil paint that I put into ready-made pendants.

MATERIALS LIST

- Good quality oil paints
- Standard resin and hardener
- Pendant blanks

TOOLS LIST

- Palette paper or white tile
- Palette knife
- Acrylic block
- Tack
- Digital scales
- Mixing cups and sticks
- Cocktail sticks
- Masking tape
- Kitchen paper

Pendant © Clare John
Knitted fabric © Trevor Collins
The Arnold family © Bob Arnold

Tips

- Use good quality oil paint. Do not economise because some colours will change or fade with time, particularly red.

- If one colour of resin is put in place and left to set/cure then it will not bleed into the next colour.

- Make more colour blends of pigments than you need and store them in an airtight container, in case you want to match them later. You may want to make earrings or other pieces of jewellery to match the pendants.

Mixing pigment into resin For basic instructions see page 20

Choose some oil paint colours that you like and put a small amount of each colour onto a white tile or palette paper. To give a wider range of colours, mix some colours together with a palette knife.

Make a resin mix with 12g standard resin and 6g hardener. Put a small amount of resin on the tile or palette paper next to each oil paint mix. Do not put it directly on the oil paint because you need to control how much paint you put in the resin. Mix the resin and a little paint with a palette knife.

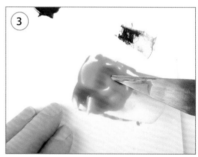

Make sure the paint and resin are thoroughly blended so that there are no streaks in the resin. Add more paint if you want the colour to be denser. The mixes can be semi transparent and you will then be able to see the texture of the pendants through them.

Mix all the colours in the same way.

Putting resin into pendants For basic instructions see page 20

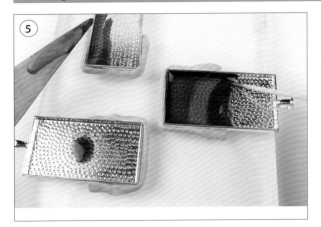

Fix the pendant blanks onto an acrylic block with tack so that they are level. Start to put the coloured resin into each pendant.

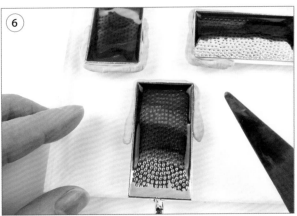

This process is quite free form. It is not possible to stop the resin colours blending a little when they join and straight lines are difficult to achieve. So just go with the flow and enjoy the effect the resins will give.

In between colours clean the palette knife with kitchen paper to keep the colours fresh.

Colour Pastes

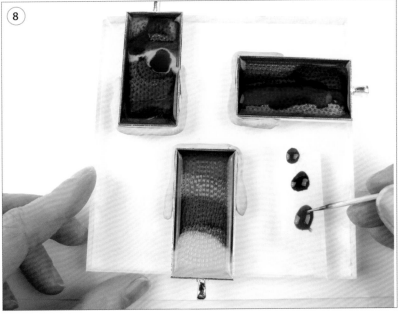

Put a test drop by the side of the pendant on a piece of masking tape. Leave the pendant to cure overnight in a warm, dust-free place. If you want, you can add a domed layer of standard resin (for instructions see page 23).

1980s
Wide Fabric and Resin Bangle

Introduction

The 1980s was a time of bold clashing colours, shoulder pads, big jewellery and post punk influences. I was inspired to design this bangle by seeing Madonna, in the film 'Desperately Seeking Susan' with her eclectic mix of fabrics and styles.

 I made this bangle by coating a strip of fabric with resin, warming it and forming it round a cylinder. I riveted the ends together to keep the resin from opening out again; resin has a 'memory' and wants to return to its original cured shape. Instead of riveting the join, you could drill and join it by linking it with jump rings.

MATERIALS LIST
- Good quality printed cotton fabric
- PVA glue and brush (I have used Mod Podge glue here)
- Standard resin and hardener
- 3mm silver tubing x 2cm

TOOLS LIST
- Bangle in your size
- Glass or jar that bangle will fit onto
- Silicone mat 20cm x 20cm
- Acrylic block 30cm x 30cm
- Digital scales
- Mixing cups and sticks
- Tape
- Silicone baking parchment
- Thin silicone baking mat (the kind that is used to roll pastry onto)
- Heat source such as an electric plate warmer or iron
- Elastic bands
- High-speed drill
- 0.8mm drill bit
- Needle files
- Steel flat plate
- Hammer
- Round punches to fit inside silver tubing
- Piercing saw and saw blades
- Planishing hammer
- Bracelet mandrel
- Respiratory mask
- Micro-mesh polishing cloths

Preparing and measuring the fabric

Find a bangle that is the right size for you and then find a drinking glass, jam jar or bottle that the bangle will fit onto. This will be the form to shape the bangle around. The form's sides need to be parallel.

Lay the printed cotton fabric on a sheet of silicone baking parchment. Using a small brush, coat the fabric on both sides with PVA glue and leave it to dry completely (PVA glue will not stick to the silicone sheet). If it is not dry, it will affect the resin curing/setting. This step is to make sure that the fabric will not fray or warp when it is cut out in Step 4.

Cut a strip of paper 35mm wide and wrap it round the form. It should overlap by at least 15mm. This is the template for the bangle.

Lay the template on the fabric in a place where you like the design. Draw round the template with a marker pen and cut out the strip of fabric.

Coating the fabric with the first layer of resin   For basic instructions see page 20

Lay the fabric strip on a silicone mat that is on an acrylic block. (Resin will not stick to the silicone mat and the acrylic block will stop everything from bending). Make a resin mix with 20g standard resin and 10g hardener.

Let it sit for 30 minutes to thicken. Coat the fabric with a deep layer of resin and put a drop of resin mix at the side as a tester. After 30 minutes check that the resin has not pulled away from the sides or seeped over the edges.

If it has, use a cocktail stick to drag resin back to the right place. Leave to cure/set in a warm, dust-free place, preferably overnight.

Coating the fabric with the second layer of resin For basic instructions see page 20

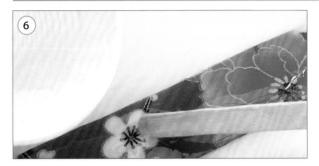

Make another resin mix with 20g standard resin and 10g hardener and coat the fabric with a second deep layer. Put another test drop at the side and leave to cure/set in a warm, dust-free place, preferably overnight.

Lift the resin coated fabric up off the silicone mat. It will come away easily.

Shaping the resin coated fabric around the form

Wrap a thin sheet of non-stick silicone baking mat around the form that you used in Step 1, and secure it with tape.

Lay the coated fabric on a piece of silicone baking parchment (this is different from the silicone mat in step 8) and put them on a gentle heat source, such as an electric plate warmer or an upside down iron set at the very lowest heat setting. Make sure it is an even heat source so that the whole length of the fabric is warmed. It should not be more than 20°C (70°F). This will take about 10 minutes.

Check whether the coated fabric is becoming flexible. Have a second strip of silicone baking parchment and some elastic bands ready for steps 12 and 13.

Lift the flexible coated fabric strip off the heat source and wrap it firmly around the form. Make sure it overlaps..

Shaping the resin coated fabric around the form continued...

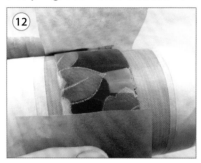

Wrap the second silicone baking parchment over the fabric.

Secure everything in place with elastic bands and leave, in a cool place, for 4 - 6 hours.

Remove the elastic bands and the silicone baking parchment.

Riveting the edges of the bangle

Put masking tape over the join on the inside of the bangle and wrap an elastic band around it to hold the bangle in position. With a high-speed drill make 3 holes where 2 layers of bangle overlap. The holes must be evenly spaced in a line parallel to the join.

Enlarge the holes with a needle file and file them so that the silver tubing will fit tightly in the holes. It must be a tight fit.

Stand the silver tube on a steel flat plate and hammer a punch into the top to flare open the tube at one end.

Fit the tubing into one of the holes with the flared open end on the inside. Make sure that the tubing cannot be pulled through the hole.

A version of this project first appeared in issue 40 of *'Making Jewellery'* magazine

Cut off the excess tubing with a piercing saw so that only about 0.5 - 0.8mm of tubing is left proud.

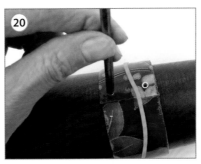

Put the bangle onto a bangle mandrel and hammer a punch into the tubing to flare open the top of the tubing that is on the outside of the bangle. Repeat Steps 16 -20 for the other 2 holes.

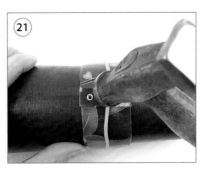

File the tubing and then planish (hammer) the edges into a good rounded surface that will not catch on clothing. Use a well-polished planishing hammer with the bangle on a bangle mandrel.

Finishing the bangle

When all 3 holes are riveted, wear a respiratory mask to rub down the edges of the bangle with Micro-mesh polishing cloths. Use the polishing cloths wet to minimise resin dust; wash the cloths afterwards. Go up the grades of polishing cloths to bring back the shine on the resin.

Polish the silver rivets inside and out, with the Micro-mesh polishing cloths, so that they do not catch on clothing or skin.

Tips

- Do not use fabric with a woven pattern. As you can see from these pictures, the design will disappear when fabric with a woven pattern is coated with resin.

Woven fabric before and after being coated with resin.

- Other fabrics, such as Angelina fibre, can be coated in resin.
- It is a good idea to store the bangle on the form, to keep the shape.

Alternative Project

I made these earrings with drilled holes at the top to put earwires through. The fabric is not formed but left flat. To make the join with the earwires more attractive, I have added 2 fake pearls.

STEAMPUNK NECKLACE

Objects and photos embedded in resin

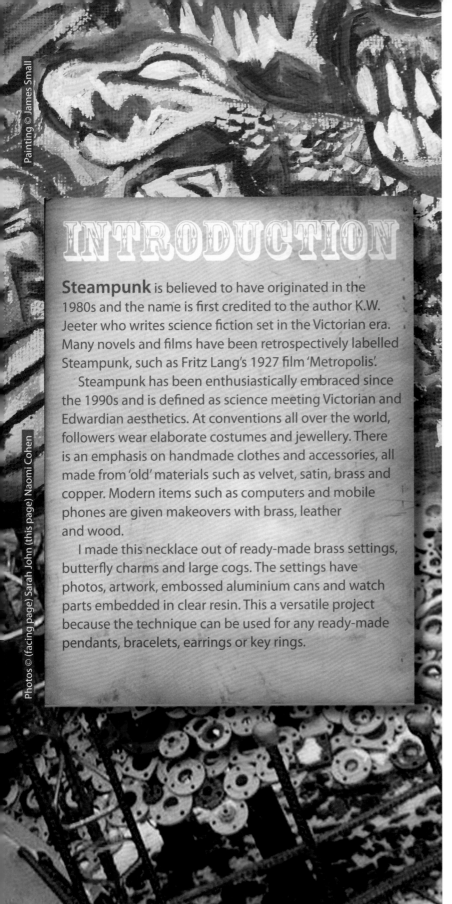

INTRODUCTION

Steampunk is believed to have originated in the 1980s and the name is first credited to the author K.W. Jeeter who writes science fiction set in the Victorian era. Many novels and films have been retrospectively labelled Steampunk, such as Fritz Lang's 1927 film 'Metropolis'.

Steampunk has been enthusiastically embraced since the 1990s and is defined as science meeting Victorian and Edwardian aesthetics. At conventions all over the world, followers wear elaborate costumes and jewellery. There is an emphasis on handmade clothes and accessories, all made from 'old' materials such as velvet, satin, brass and copper. Modern items such as computers and mobile phones are given makeovers with brass, leather and wood.

I made this necklace out of ready-made brass settings, butterfly charms and large cogs. The settings have photos, artwork, embossed aluminium cans and watch parts embedded in clear resin. This a versatile project because the technique can be used for any ready-made pendants, bracelets, earrings or key rings.

MATERIALS LIST

- Aluminium can
- Photos on high quality photo paper
- Old hardback book for text
- PVA glue
- Brass settings with a jump ring x 18
- 2 part epoxy glue
- Low viscosity resin and hardener
- Watch cogs
- Butterfly charms
- Standard resin and hardener
- Copper jump rings
- Copper ring and bar clasp

TOOLS LIST

- Scissors
- Heatproof mat
- Small soldering torch or cooking torch
- Embossing tool
- Abrasive paper
- Silcone baking parchment
- Computer, scanner and printer
- Digital scales
- Mixing cups
- Mixing sticks
- Cocktail sticks
- Acrylic block
- Tack

Preparing the artwork to go into the settings

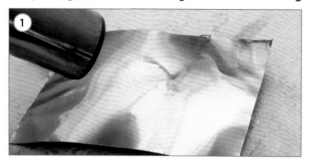

Cut the aluminium can open and cut out a rectangle about 8cm x 10cm. Heat it gently with a torch on a heatproof mat. This will soften the metal and burn off the plastic coating giving the surface a lovely brass colour.

Using an embossing tool or a ballpoint pen, draw a design on the printed side of the metal. This project has a spider's web drawing but it can be anything you like.

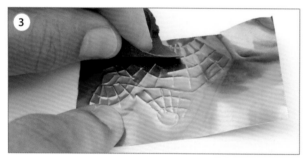

Turn the metal over and rub the drawing lightly with some abrasive paper. This will highlight the drawing and contrast it with the brass colour of the metal.

Find an image that you like; I have used a skull painting here. Scan it and size it to fit the brass links. Duplicate the image several times and print it on high quality photo paper. Cut out one of the images to be a template for the other artwork you will be using. Check that it fits the brass setting.

Using your template cut out several circles from the metal can.

Seal a page from an old book with 2 layers of PVA glue on each side. If you put the page on some silicone baking parchment, it will not get stuck. Leave to dry completely. When it is dry, use your template to cut out several circles, choosing wording that you like.

Cut out several photo images, in this case the skulls, and seal them with PVA glue. Leave to dry completely.

Cut out another image; here I have used photos of eyes that have been printed on photo paper and I have added different tints to the images on the computer. Seal and leave to dry as in Steps 6 and 7.

Making the settings and gluing in the artwork

Make 9 settings by gluing 18 brass settings together, with 2 part epoxy glue, so that they are Double-sided.

Glue different images and metal circles into one side of the 9 links with 2 part epoxy glue. Vary them as you wish. I have 3 eyes, 2 metal circles, 2 skulls and 2 texts.

TIPS

- Research your images (I have used some taken from a painting by my son, James Small, and photos of my nephew, Joshua John's eyes). Remember copyright issues when using images.
- Tint the base resin to give a sepia effect to the images.
- Use different size links to change the dynamic of the necklace.

Putting the first resin layer into one side of the settings   For basic instructions see page 20

When the glue is dry, fix the settings, with the images facing up, onto an acrylic block using tack. Make sure they are level and that no tack goes over the edge of the link.

Make a mix of 4g low viscosity resin and 2g hardener and put a thin layer of resin mix into each setting.

Add butterfly charms and watch cogs to the settings with a cocktail stick.

Cover with a tiny amount of resin mix to ensure they will be fixed in place. Put a test drop of resin on masking tape on the side. Leave to cure/set in a warm, dust-free place but not on a source of direct heat as this would make the paper give out air and you would get bubbles in the resin.

Domed resin in settings   For basic instructions see page 20

When the first layer of resin is hard enough to touch, make a mix of 4g standard resin and 2g of hardener. Put a high layer in each setting; it should look like a glass lens on top of each image. Put a test drop of resin on masking tape on the side.

Standard resin tends to generate bubbles so put the acrylic block with the settings onto a heatproof mat and pass a soft flame quickly over the surface of the resin. This will draw the bubbles out of the resin mix. Leave to cure/set in a warm, dust-free place, preferably overnight. Do not place on a source of direct heat as this would make the paper give out air and you would get bubbles in the resin.

Putting the artwork and resin into the reverse of the settings For basic instructions see page 20

Turn the settings over and fix to a ring shaped piece of tack. This will make it easier to level the settings now that they have resin inside. Repeat Steps 10 to 16 on the other sides. You can choose to match the images on the reverse or not.

Assembling the necklace

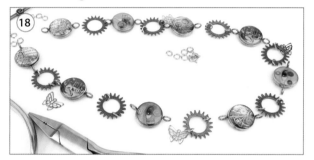

When the resin is completely cured/set, assemble the necklace in a sequence you like. Put the cog charms in between each brass setting and add butterfly charms to some of the cogs.

Link the components with copper jump rings and fix a copper ring and bar fitting to each end.

Objects and photos embedded in resin

Industrial Chic Bangle

Cast resin bangle filled with objects

Photo © Clare John

Introduction

Industrial Chic can be seen as a development of Steampunk, from 2010 on. Industrial Chic interior design reclaims industrial furniture and machinery and reuses it in domestic settings. For example, a kitchen might have filing cabinets that have been sprayed silver (or even left with the original rust as a feature) as kitchen units. Fashion design uses industrial chic by adopting industrial imagery and logos for clothing. The look is "edgy" – a reclamation of manufactured items.

In this bangle, I have used items that would normally be thrown away. I was looking at the design of ephemera such as bank cards; a lot of thought has gone into their design and it seemed a shame to get rid of them. So I have 're-purposed' these items by setting them in clear resin in a silicone bangle mould. I have also included circuit boards from defunct digital scales and the chips from phone SIM cards.

MATERIALS LIST
- Low viscosity resin and hardener
- Out of date credit cards, circuit boards, SIM cards; whatever you like
- Standard resin and hardener
- Silicone bangle mould

TOOLS LIST
- Heavy duty scissors or snips
- Acrylic block
- Digital scales
- Plastic cups
- Mixing sticks
- Cocktail sticks
- Tack
- Masking tape
- Respiratory mask
- Wet and dry abrasive paper- 280 grit is fine

Preparing items to go inside the bangle

Cut the pieces that you want to use so they fit the silicone bangle mould; check that they do not stick up out of the mould.

Making the first resin mix For basic instructions see page 20

Stand the bangle mould on the acrylic block to keep it firm and steady. Make a mix of 6g low viscosity resin and 3g hardener. Pour some into the bangle mould so that there is about 2 or 3mm of resin at the bottom. Leave in a warm, dust-free place for about 30 minutes.

Keep checking to see if the resin has started to cure. When the resin has become tacky and pulls when you put a cocktail stick in it, it is ready for the next step. Be careful that it does not set too much or you will not be able to do Step 4.

Push the cut up pieces from Step 1 into the tacky resin. This means that they will not swim about and float.

Making and pouring the second resin mix For basic instructions see page 20

Make a second resin mix with 20g low viscosity resin and 10g hardener. Mix well and pour to the top of the bangle mould. Check for pockets of air trapped behind any of the inserted pieces and pop bubbles with a pin. Do not be tempted to pass a flame over this bangle because the material that the inserts are made from might be flammable at a low temperature.

Leave to cure/set in a warm, dust-free place, preferably overnight. Put the mould and casting into the refrigerator for 30 minutes. Then gently ease the bangle out of the mould.

Rubbing down the bangle

Wear a respiratory mask and rub down the top of the casting on wet and dry abrasive paper; use it wet. Rub the casting down until it is level and no shiny areas are left. Wash the abrasive paper afterwards to get rid of the dust.

Making the third and fourth resin mixes For basic instructions see page 20

Fix the bangle to an acrylic block with tack and double check that it is level. This is very important as you are going to put resin on it. Make a mix of 4g standard resin and 2 g hardener. Put a domed layer around the surface that has been rubbed down – this will bring back the shine and give a comfortable surface to wear against your wrist. Leave to cure/set in a warm, dust-free place, preferably overnight. Put a tester drop of resin onto some masking tape.

Repeat Step 7 and 8 on the other side of the bangle - so that both sides have a gentle curved surface.

Tips

- Anything can be embedded as long as it is bone dry.
- If you cannot find a suitable silicone bangle mould, you could make one using a shop bought bangle as a master (see 1960s Fluorescent Ring project page 86).
- Add text or pictures printed onto acetate sheet to give an added story to the bangle

Gallery 4

1 **Sue Rennie** The 'What came first' Necklace, 2013.
   *Resin, quail's egg, Haematite, Howlite bird, seed beads
   and handmade wire clasp.* Photo by the artist.
2 **Wilde Works Contemporary Jewellery**
   *Kinetic Chameleon-Eye Rings, 2012.
   Silver and resin.* Photo by Paul Mounsey.
3 **Wendy Jo New** Drink Jewellery, 2003.
   Silver, resin and dry pigment. Photo by Dean Powell.

4 **Meghan Wagg** Orange Larynx Pendant, 2012.
Silver and resin.
5 **Meghan Wagg** Red Domed Pendant, 2010.
Silver and resin.
Photos by the artist.

Gallery 4

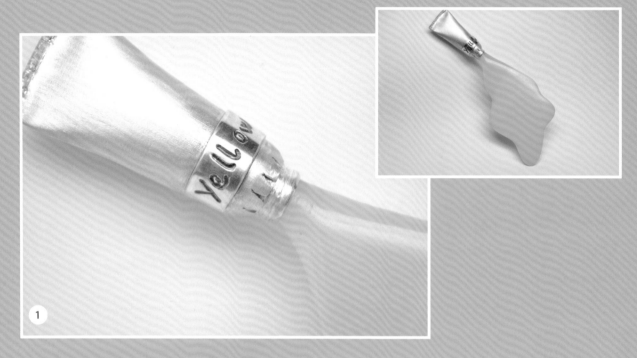

1 **Melania Zucchi** Yellow Gouache Brooch, 2013.
Silver and resin.
Photos by the artist.

3 **Saskia Poller** Ives Family Collage Picture, 2012.
Resin, photos, lace, cotton tape, sequins and beads.
Photo by Paul Mounsey.

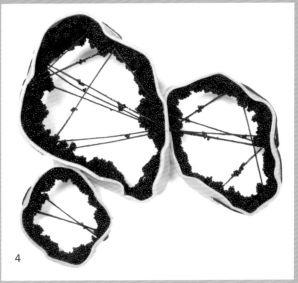

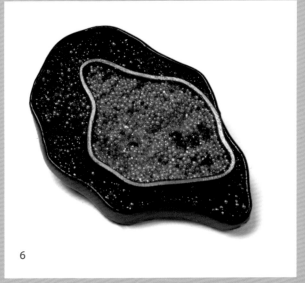

3 **Jessica Armstrong** Growth, 2013.
Silver, resin, cubic zirconia, microbeads and glitter.

4 **Jessica Armstrong** Connected Brooch, 2013.
Powder coated brass, resin, thread and microbeads.
Photos by Erin Cora Turner.

5 **Jessica Armstrong** Drip, 2014.
Powder coated neckwire, resin, microbeads, glitter and flocking fibres. Photo by Nash Quinn.

6 **Jessica Armstrong** Exposed, 2013.
Powder coated brass, resin, black spinnel, glitter and black microbeads. Photo by Erin Cora Turner.

Glossary

Acrylic sheet Acrylic sheet or block used to support jewellery items or moulds while resin is setting. The best thickness is 10mm because then it is not likely to bend when warm. Trade names are Perspex (UK) and Plexiglass (USA).

Anneal To soften metal by heating and quenching it (plunging it into cold water while it is still hot). Look at *Complete Metalsmith* by Tim McCreight for more details.

Bangle mandrel A tapered steel form for making bangles. Mandrels come in different profiles - round, oval or square.

Barrel polisher Also known as a Tumbler or Tumble Polisher. This is a plastic cylinder with removable caps each end, which contains metal pins or beads (known as shot), water and special soap. One end is removed and jewellery is put in and the cylinder is re-sealed. Then it is put onto a machine, which turns it and the shot is thrown against the jewellery and polishes it by abrasion.

Barrier cream A cream that forms a protective barrier on the skin. It should be applied at regular intervals when working with resin. It is an alternative to wearing gloves. I prefer barrier cream because gloves can get holes in and it is much worse for your skin, if resin and hardener get inside the gloves.

Binding wire Thin flexible iron wire, which is used to hold pieces of metal together while soldering. The iron will not bond to silver solder so it can be removed after soldering. Do not put iron into safety pickle as a chemical reaction happens that will copper-plate other metals in the pickle.

Bronze powder Super fine particles of bronze. It is essential to wear a mask when using this powder as it is easily inhaled and can damage lungs. It is also highly inflammable. Download health and safety instructions here **http://www.tiranti.co.uk/ EdgeImpactShop/HealthAndSafetyDocs/510-040. pdf?rnd=2014-07-25%2008:52:41**

Buff stick A strip of wood with abrasive paper wrapped round it and secured with tape.

Cabochons A cabochon is a stone with a smooth, curved and polished surface that is different from a faceted stone, which has different flat surfaces cut into it.

Catches This means different types of clasps to fasten necklaces, chains and bracelets.

Cloisonné An enamelling technique where wire enclosures are made to contain different colours of enamel. This is good method for separating resin colours so that they do not bleed into each other. The wires can be glued or soldered.

Cold enamel This is just another name for resin. It can look like traditional hot enamel but hot enamel is a very different process, which involves firing glass powders on jewellery, in a kiln.

Contact glue This glue is spread on each surface that is to be glued together and left to dry a little. Then when the two sides are put together, they will stick immediately.

Cure Another term for setting. This resin cures or sets when it is mixed with hardener.

De-gassing Removing bubbles from resin or silicone. This can be done in a vacuum chamber machine or by passing a gentle flame over the surface but only if there are no flammable materials proud of the resin surface.

Dividers look like an old fashioned compass for drawing circles. They are used to mark metal and plastic, either in circles or parallel lines.

Dremel The trade name for an electric tool that can be used for drilling, polishing and sanding on a small scale. Jewellers also use a tool called a flexible shaft for the same purposes.

Earring wires Wire hooks for hanging earrings from pierced ears.

Epoxy glue This is a 2-part glue, one part is resin and the other is hardener. They must be mixed thoroughly and will set in the time stated on the packet. A 5-minute epoxy is used in this book. Epoxy glue is compatible with all the epoxy resins.

Exothermic reaction A reaction in which heat is given off, such as when resin and hardener are mixed together.

Findings The name given to jewellery components such as jump rings, catches and earring wires.

Gaffer tape Also known as duct tape. It is a very sticky tape that is removed easily without leaving a tacky surface. It is useful in making a mould box when other types of tape will lose their stickiness in contact with liquid silicone mould material.

Gel Resin This is the common name for thixotropic resin. It is a very thick resin, which will not drip off curved surfaces. It is used in rings and bangles as well as domed surfaces.

Gilding flake Imitation gold leaf, which is very thin pieces of gold-coloured foil.

Inside ring felt Ring felt cone for polishing the insides of rings. (I find it very handy for holding rings while I polish the outside, as my fingers do not get too hot holding the ring this way).

Jig The name given to something that you bend wire or metal around to repeat a shape each time.

Jump rings Small metal rings made by wrapping wire round a metal cylinder to make a long spring. They are cut into separate rings, which are useful to link things together , such as chain to catches. They can be used for making cloisonné compartments.

Low viscosity resin The best resin for pouring into moulds, as it will fill all tiny areas of a mould.

Mandrel A form around which metal is shaped.

Masking tape Adhesive tape used by artists to mask off areas to be protected. The adhesive is made so that it peels off easily and does not stick too firmly.

Master This is the name for an original item that is used to make a mould. Resin is poured into the mould and a copy of the master is made.

Meniscus Is the name given to the curve in the upper surface of a liquid.

Micro- mesh polishing cloths These are useful abrasive cloths in different grades from coarse to extremely fine. They were developed for the airplane industry and are good for polishing resin, glass, metal, wood and acrylic sheet.

Mould box A container or wall around a master. Silicone mould material is poured into to it. Then the mould box is removed when the silicone is set.

Non-slip matting This is found in kitchen shops and hardware stores. It is flexible non-slip latex matting used to stop things moving on shelves.

Palette knife Flexible metal or plastic knife commonly used by artists. It is used to mix pigments thoroughly into resin.

Parallel pliers Pliers with jaws that open in parallel lines rather than hinging to a 'V' shape.

Pickle Also known as safety pickle. This is a very weak acid solution that will clean up metal after it has been soldered. To pickle something is to put it in the pickle until it is clean.

Piercing saw Jewellers' saw which uses very fine saw

Glossary

blades for cutting out metal.

Pin vice A very useful small tool. It has different sized chucks (grips which hold different sized drill bits or pins).

Planish To planish metal is to give it a smooth finish by hammering it with a special hammer called a planishing hammer. This hammer has polished surfaces so the metal is not scarred. It is a smoothing technique and is usually done with the metal sitting on a hard surface, for example, a steel plate.

Plasticene Modelling compound that is readily available. It contains sulphur so it must not be used when making silicone moulds, as it will stop the silicone curing properly.

Plastic tubing This is used in hospitals and is also ideal for setting into resin to create a channel for elastic, cord or wire. It avoids having to drill through resin.

Plastilene A sulphur free kind of plasticene. It must be used with silicone mould material as sulphur stops the silicone curing properly.

Polishing cloths You can buy cloths impregnated with polish, which will clean silver.

Post cure When a silicone mould is made, it is best to remove the mould box and master and put the mould to cure at a minimum temperature of 30ºC (86ºF) for another 3 - 4 hours. This will make the mould harder and longer lasting.

PVA glue (Polyvinyl acetate) White glue, which is commonly used by schools, wood workers, scrap bookers and bookbinders. It is also known as wood glue and (in the USA) as Elmer's Glue. A brand name is Mod Podge.

Quenching Plunging a hot piece of metal into cold water to cool it down instantly.

Ring mandrel A form (usually round and tapered in steel) around which a ring is hammered into shape.

RTV silicone (Room Temperature Vulcanising silicone) This is a two-part silicone mould material, which consists of a base material and a curative material. It starts as two liquids and cures into a hard rubber at room temperature. There is a hardness range known as a shore range; from soft (15 shore) to hard (40 shore). A hardness of 20 shore is ideal for resin casting.

Set This resin sets or cures when it is mixed with hardener.

Silicone baking parchment This is found in kitchen shops and is normally used for baking. Resin does not stick to it so it is very useful (see project 14).

Silicone baking mat This is also found in kitchen shops. It is used for covering the bottom of baking tins and pastry can be rolled on it.

Silicone mat A mat made from RTV silicone, which has been poured into a flat backed rectangular box. An ideal thickness is 15mm.

Soldering wig An iron wire pad for supporting the article to be soldered with minimum heat dispersion.

Standard resin/doming resin This is more viscous or thicker than casting or enamelling resin. The difference will not be visible to the naked eye but it has a greater ability to build a high domed surface on resin projects.

Steel wool Fine soft filaments of steel in a bundle. It is used as a gentle abrasive on wood, metal, glass and paintwork. It comes in different grades.

Super Glue This is a trade name for cyanoacrylate glue. It sticks things instantly but it should not be used with epoxy resin as they are not compatible. It will react with epoxy resin and the glue will not work after a short time.

T Cut A gentle abrasive paste used to clean car paintwork. (USA equivalent is 3M Rubbing Compound) It is perfect for gently polishing resin surfaces that are slightly scratched.

Tack Stretchy sticky compound that is used to stick things to walls or other surfaces temporarily. It has trade names such as Blu Tack (in the UK) and ArtMinds™ Crafty Tack Reusable Adhesive (in the USA).

Tester A drop of resin mix put beside projects that can be tested to see if the resin mix is properly set or cured. This prevents the project from damage.

Thixotropic Resin Also known as gel resin. This is a very thick resin, which will not drip off curved surfaces. It is used in rings and bangles as well as domed surfaces. It is also known as gel resin.

Triblet Another name for a ring mandrel.

Viscosity The name given to the thickness or glueyness of a liquid.

Vitreous enamel Traditional glass enamel that is made from finely ground glass powders on metal, which are fired in a very hot kiln to fuse them to the metal.

Vonax The trade name for a polishing compound designed to polish plastics on a large polishing motor. (USA equivalent Plastic-Color Compound or Dynuba 171).

Wet and dry paper Abrasive paper that can be used wet or dry. When wet it keeps the dust to a minimum.

Suppliers

United Kingdom

Resin and allied materials

Resin8
www.resin8.co.uk
01242 602739

RF Bright Enterprises Ltd
www.rfbright.co.uk
01622 717141

Tiranti
www.tiranti.co.uk
0845 123 2100
Supplier of Bronze Filler Powder

Tools

Cookson
www.cooksongold.com
0845 100 1122

Kernowcraft
www.kernowcraft.com
01872 573888

Suttons
www.suttontools.co.uk
0121 236 7139

Walsh
www.hswalsh.com
01959 543 660

Silver

Cookson
www.cooksongold.com
0845 100 1122

Kernowcraft
www.kernowcraft.com
01872 573888

Silver rings for gel resin

Resin8
www.resin8.co.uk
01242 602739

Beads and threading materials

Jewellery Maker
www.jewellerymaker.com
0800 6444 655

PJ Beads
www.beads.co.uk
01704 575461

Kernowcraft
www.kernowcraft.com
01872 573888

Riverside Beads
www.riversidebeads.co.uk
01778 346810

Copper blanks

Cookson
www.cooksongold.com
0845 100 1122

CJ Beaders
www.cjbeaders.co.uk
01425 279992

Silver plated blanks and jewellery mounts

Resin8
www.resin8.co.uk
01242 602739

United States

Resin and other materials

Rio Grande
www.riogrande.com
800-545-6566

Michaels
www.michaels.com
1-800-642-4235

Resin Obsession
www.resinobsession.com
info@resinobsession.com

Tools

Rio Grande
www.riogrande.com
800-545-6566

Beads and tools

Beadaholique
www.beadaholique.com
service@beadaholique.com

Silver plated blanks and jewellery mounts

Firemountain Gems
www.firemountaingems.com
1-800-355-2137

Bronze filler powders

www.ebay.com

Bibliography

Adelson, Debra (2008) *The Art of Jewelry Plastic and Resin* New York, Lark Books

Campbell, Jean (2009) *Steampunk Style Jewelry* Minneapolis, Creative Publishing International Inc

Codina, Carlos (2005) *The New Jewelry* New York, Lark Books

Haab, Sherri (2006) *The Art of Resin Jewelry* New York, Watson-Guptil Publications

Haab, Sherri, Haab, Rachel, Haab, Michelle, (2011) *The Art of Resin Clay* New York, Potter Craft

Hughes, Graham (1972) *The Art of Jewelry* New York, The Viking Press Inc

Kühnemann, Ursula (1969) *Cold Enamelling* London, Mills & Boon Ltd

Lenart Kazmer, Susan (2011) *Making Connections* California, Interweave Press Ltd

Mack, John (ed) (1988) *Ethnic Jewellery* London, British Museum Press

McCreight, Tim (2004) *The Complete Metalsmith* Portland, Brynmorgen Press, Inc

Murphy, Kathie (2002) *Resin Jewellery* London, A&C Black

Murphy, Kathie (2009) *Design and Make Non-Precious Jewellery* London, A&C Black

Peck, Denise and Dickerson, Jane (2011) *Hand Crafted Wire Findings* Loveland, Interweave Press Ltd

Phillips, Clare (2008) *Jewels and Jewellery* London, V&A Publishing

Robinson, Kristen (2011) *Tales of Adornment* Cincinnati, North Light Books

Tait, Hugh (ed) (1986) *Seven Thousand years of Jewellery* London, British Museums Publications

Wicks, Sylvia (1985) *Jewellery Making Manual* London, Quill Publishing

Wilkinson, Kerry (2009) *Create your own Resin Jewellery* Peterborough, PennyDog Publications

www.merriam-webster.com/dictionary/bronze%20age

(accessed 21 June 2013)

www.madaboutthehouse.com/we-like-this-industrial-chic

(accessed 21 June 2013)

Kumihimo braid: www.youtube.com/watch?v=2I_uAC_Mxfw

(accessed 5 August 2013)

en.wikipedia.org/wiki/Mesopotamia

(accessed 30 March 2013)

http://www.mysteriousetruscans.com/lifestyle.html

(accessed 11 June 2013)

http://en.wikipedia.org/wiki/Lord_of_Sipán

(accessed 22 June 2013)

http://en.wikipedia.org/wiki/Art_Nouveau

(accessed 30 June 2013)

http://en.wikipedia.org/wiki/Bronze_Age

(accessed 2 July 2013)

http://en.wikipedia.org/wiki/Art_Deco

(accessed 5 July 2013)

http://www.allaboutgemstones.com/gem_history.html

(accessed 9 December 2012)

Index

www.resin8.co.uk
info@resin8.co.uk

THREE GABLES
Publishing